BREAKING THROUGH
THE 4 BARRIERS
TO QUALITY

Building Business Infrastructures

BRUCE SNELL

Published By:
Ordway Anderson Publishing
149 NW Columbia Court
Chapin, South Carolina 29036

Internet Address HTTP:\\www.brucesnell.com
e-mail address: bsnell@bsg-international.com

Applied Business Science, Awareness Center
Quality Awareness Council
BaseWork Systems 2000 (BW/S)
Building Business Infrastructures
BaseWork Center (BW/C)
The Four Barriers To Quality
BSG Awareness Center
BaseValues
BaseSkills
Virtual Corporation

Library of Congress Catalog Card Number: 97-094436
ISBN: 1-4392-3191-5
ISBN-13: 9781439231913

Dedication

With love and thanks, I dedicate this work to my wife, friend and co-worker of many years, Karen. Thanks for the support, belief in me and hard work that have made me who I am today. Thanks also to the daughter of my dreams, Hayden "Mookie," the girl with the smile of life.

The BaseWork Systems 2000 would not be possible without Jim Andreoli, Sr. and his belief in me and the BW/S 2000 concept. Yes, Jim, Sr., you did help with the book. Additionally, I would like to thank the coordinators in training for working through the tough times with me. Thanks, Jim Andreoli, Jr., Tony Andreoli, and Andy Andreoli. Also a big thank you goes out to Maxine Taylor for her developmental work on the project and to all the employees of Baker Commodities, Inc. Thanks, you made this possible!

A very special group deserves a big Thank You:

the Ordways, the Bradys, the Lantzs, the Vaughns, the Harshas, the Morrows, the Smiths, the Andreolis, Stan Fenn, Emeka and Pastor Ke Ena — and of course, Nick Anderson.

Thanks also to my parents, Sharon and Gerald Snell, plus the Snell clan from Opp and Mobile Bay Alabama, to the Mountains of North Georgia. Thanks also to my Castine Maine family, the Ordways. Special thoughts and thanks to B.B. and Kent Snell.

I also want to acknowledge and thank all of the folks that as friends supported the "grass roots movement":

the Carricos, David Rasmussen, the Stuckers, the Bonins, Pam Everett, Lincoln Annas, the Nermers, Steve Yamagouchi, Martha Ward, Steve Fryer, Fred Fourcher, Dale Goff, Jr., the Youngbloods, the Aldridges, Darla

Salin, Tim Parker, the Harbert, Goodman, McKenzie, Leski, and McLeod families.

I would like to also thank all of the friends that, over the years, have believed in me and supported every goal I have achieved: Stan Fenn, Victor Israel, Carsten Ecks, Don Trimble, the Bakers, Bob Taylor, Marvin Ash, the Odgers, Coaches Bacon, Perrin, Biggs, and Clune, the McCullys, the Rayyis family, and the Bristols.

I especially want to thank the person that started my career in Quality: Mike Smith and the Smith family— Jeanne, Kerry, Mike, Sandy and Megan.

Endorsements

"If you're looking for a solution to your Quality woes – stop here! This book is all you need. Bruce Snell has created one of the most innovative and practical approaches to achieving performance and product excellence. Whether you're a small town business or global market competitor, you can "do it better" by following Bruce's ingenious process."

— Victor Wright

Performance Excellence Functional Learning Lead, Raytheon & On-Line Faculty, Chapman University, Organizational Leadership Department

"Often overlooked in the 'do more and do it faster' business world that we live in today are two fundamental principles: 1. Perform your job to the best of your abilities and 2. Treat others as you would like to be treated. In The 4 Barriers To Quality, Mr. Snell lays the framework for creating a culture in the workplace that embodies these two virtues. He does this by emphasizing the importance of having a sound infrastructure where information is constantly being obtained, interpreted, communicated and formally trained in an environment that is open and responsive to feedback. This book is a quick and easy read filled with practical steps that will transform the way your organization does business."

—Matthew H. Frick, MS, OTR/L, CWCE

Director of Business Development
The Moore Orthopaedic Clinic, PA

"In order for any business, large or small to succeed in today's dynamic environment, behavioral and cultural changes are a must. *Breaking Through The 4 Barriers To Quality* is a straight-forward approach to creating the required changes."

— Larry J. Enders

President and CEO, Oliver Rubber Company

"The principles and practices given in **_The 4 Barriers to Quality_** are foundational, practical and profoundly needed for effectiveness in and out of the workplace. This is not "nice to know information" – it is _critical_ to learn and apply _now_ for operational success in today's dynamic world. Bruce's experience and down to earth approach are received well by all groups and industries. I cannot recommend this book and program highly enough."

— Mandy Roberts
Consulting Business Owner and Public Education Teacher

"The business world of the new millennium requires a commitment to quality, integrity and the individual worker. Bruce Snell not only identifies the problem that impeded personal and organizational growth, he has created **THE** program that will put renewed life into the business world. Bruce's program, emphasizing ethics and integrity, is a refreshing change from "bottom line" management. _Breaking Through The 4 Barriers To Quality_ promises to be a catalyst that will improve our quality of life in the new millennium...A must-read for everyone in an organization!"

— Pamela Everett
President, Gem Legal Management, Inc.

"For many years, I have believed that the approach to business problem-solving and continuous improvement that Bruce Snell advocates, is very effective. In this book, he provides examples of how and why it works in real business settings...I eagerly await the "how to" detail of **BaseWork Systems 2000**."

— M.A. Stimpert
Senior Vice President, Planning and Administration, Gold Kist, Inc.

"Finally, a book which addresses the problems of quality rather than just the symptomatic issues."

— Dr. Michael Gallagher
President, Mesa State College, Colorado

"Bruce Snell provides a refreshingly, humanistic, and ethical approach to building business infrastructure in an age of unrelenting cartoon-sarcasm about management. Watch out *Dilbert*, *Breaking Through The 4 Barriers To Quality* will take the horns off of your bosses' head!"

— Fred Fourcher
CEO, Miralite Communications

Bruce...What can I say. Finally a program that if it is followed will identify the problems in a company and has the solutions and means to correct those problems. A job well done.

— James Andreoli
President, Baker Commodities, Inc.

"When I'm not on the road touring with **BTO**, I'm following Bruce Snell's Book, *Breaking Through The 4 Barriers To Quality*, to make sure I'm '**Taking Care Of Business**' properly."

— C.F. Turner
(Formerly) Bachman Turner Overdrive Winnipeg Canada

"Bruce's background is that of a common man for which he is proud. However, *Breaking Through The 4 Barriers To Quality* is that of genius our generation has not experienced. Where have all our leaders gone? I'm not sure, but the qualities and achievements of Bruce Snell personifies leadership."

— Ted Carrico
President National Association of Postmasters of the United States

"Finally, someone has taken time to figure out the detailed process of implementing quality in American business. Bruce Snell is leading the crusade for quality in America."

— Nick Anderson
Executive Director, Mesa Research Institute & Adjunct Professor
University of Southern California

"Today I finished reading your book, *Breaking Through The 4 Barriers To Quality*, and I am convinced that every company in the world with employees or companies that contemplate having employees should have the privilege of reading this book. Even though I have had two years with it-as I was a part of a rather large company that you instituted this system in-I found the book very interesting and easy to read. So much so that I did not want to put it down".

— Tom Vaughn
Ridge Creek Ranch
Nowata, Oklahoma

"This book is right on target for those looking for the means to identify the problems related to quality and also the solutions."

— Mike Smith
Plant Manager
Southern California, Treadco Inc.

"America needs *The 4 Barriers to Quality*! Having worked with many different companies throughout my professional career, I have seen every day the frustrations employees within companies experience because they do not have the principles Bruce has laid out in this book. If these principles were implemented in corporate America, we would—without a doubt—become the most competitive and efficient country in the world, and at the same time, our employees would enjoy their work because the frustrations of the workplace would be virtually eliminated."

— Roger Spires
Sales Manager
Ferguson Heating and Cooling

A Positive Note

"For every process action there is a people reaction affecting the whole system"

Bruce

QUALITY G.R.I.T

We all share a desire to belong to vibrant organizations with integrity, impact and the time to enjoy the fruits of our labor. This quality organization, BSG "discovered", has four objectives with common characteristics, which are:

Growth of our organization
- Employees growing personally and professionally
- Process(es) that are functional
- The ability to change

Retain the integrity
- Of our organization's name
- Of our product and/or service
- Of our work environment

Impact of our organization
- With our customers and employees
- Community and family
- Raising the bar of quality in our industry

Time restraints that affect
- Balance between family and work
- Quality of life at work and home
- Quality time spent wisely

These organization's characteristics, we call the "Quality G.R.I.T." Throughout this book think of how the 4 Barriers To Quality impact your 'Quality Bottom Line'.

QUALITY© DISCIPLINES

Quality© Awareness: This awareness of The 4 Barriers To Quality© and the Ten Quality© Disciplines should apply to our everyday life at home and at work. The disciplines and habits are guidelines as we provide our product/service to both our internal/external suppliers/customers.

1 **Quality Definition**: Quality contributes and/or increases the well-being of others by meeting and/or exceeding our Agreement of Quality

2 **Agreement of Quality** – Quality is best defined in written form and beneficial for all parties. We are morally and ethically bound by our verbal and written promises and agreements. The example of written is the following; contract, system, procedure, policy and order/request. The verbal example is your word.

3 **Commitment** – An assurance that one will do what was agreed upon in regards to terms/conditions, events/actions of agreement of trust of performance.

4 **Guarantee** – A firm promise to perform to the agreement and commitment of quality.

5 **Truth** – The accuracy, sincerity, integrity. The performance of the agreement.

6 **Trust** – The acceptance, confidence and/or security of agreement as true or reliable and based on a performance relationship.

7 **Trustworthiness** – To have faith/belief to honor the Agreement of Quality. This includes yourself, events/actions and your products/services.

8 **Continuance and Growth** – To endure our current events/actions of your daily life, at home and at work. In the same breath we need to grow our minds and characters. This discipline insures our quality of life and our organization's product/service

9 **Contributes** – To give to others/society quality that benefits and/or makes life better; "the quality purpose".

10 **Well-being** – Quality discipline contributes to health, happiness, welfare, prosperity and adds to our quality of life.

A Positive Note

Leadership must lead change and communicate that change with all the employees. The employees are powerless to change without a system.

Bruce

TABLE OF CONTENTS IN-BRIEF

A Positive Note

Communication must be encouraged and modeled by leadership. Communication that is to be held accountable must be in written form.

Bruce

COMPLETE TABLE OF CONTENTS

Chapter 1   BREAKING THROUGH FEAR

Chapter 2 LACK OF COMMUNICATION

Chapter 3 LACK OF WRITTEN PROCEDURE

Chapter 4 LACK OF TRAINING

Chapter 5 ORGANIZATINAL CHANGE

Chapter 6 GETTING STARTED

Chapter 7 BASESKILLS OF EMPLOYEES

Chapter 8 DEFINING YOUR JOB:

THE BASEWORK CENTER CONCEPT

Chapter 9 DEFINING ORGANIZATIONAL SYSTEMS

Chapter 10 FOUR PROBLEM SOLVING PROCESSES

Chapter 11 CONTINUOUS IMPROVEMENT

Chapter 12 MORE STORIES

(Including placement listing for all stories)

Chapter One

Chapter Eight

Chapter Nine   . . . .

Chapter Ten

Chapter Eleven

Chapter Twelve

Chapter 13   LIFE'S LESSONS

A Positive Note

Agents of change recognize that change is inevitable; therefore change is now but ever processing.

As agents of change you will lead the organization by removing fear, opening communication, defining procedure and formalizing training.

Bruce

Foreword

Exceeding the expectations of your customers is smart business practice. Smart business practices are what Bruce Snell captures in his book.

Providing leadership is a very challenging undertaking. Providing quality related leadership becomes even more challenging in today's and tomorrow's society and economy. Bruce Snell's book, The 4 Barriers to Quality, provides an opportunity to develop comprehensive, efficient, and effective processes that will enable an individual and/or organization to ostensibly deal with the 4 barriers to quality found in the infrastructure of every organization:

1. Fear of expression and/or actions.
2. Lack of communication (verbal and/or written).
3. Lack of written procedure.
4. Lack of training.

The author has provided a toolkit of activities that are designed to strengthen an organization's quality management strategy. The power of this approach is well documented in the underlying research.

This book is written for quality specialists, academics, and leaders in business, industry, and government. The wisdom in this book is grounded in real experiences and practices. I have had the opportunity of teaching and consulting with Bruce in various corporate and team environments, and have witnessed the breakthrough possibilities and probabilities available through the processes and techniques he teaches and advocates to others.

I have read many leadership and quality management related books over the past forty years, with this book and this author leaving me with a very positive impression and process. I am confident, by the time you finish this book, you will have the same positive impression.

— Michael A. Demma
President, Demma Consulting

A Positive Note

When we try to manage our people by quotas or line-item management (management by the numbers) an employee fights a daily battle with insecurity and fear.

The reason we use line-item management is because, in the past we were taught to "hit the numbers". The question is, can the line-item number be trusted?

What we should have been taught was how to show improvement through our process and people. This will improve the bottom line.

Bruce

Preface - A Case Study

Quality has no Borders

Emeka C. Ene
Chief Executive Officer,
Oildata
Port Harcourt, Nigeria

We implemented BSG's "4-barriers to Quality" program in 2004, at our company, Oildata Wireline Services. Oildata is located in Port Harcourt, Nigeria, a bustling oil producing country in West Africa, usually in the news for the wrong reasons.

Our company had been growing at over 30% annually for the previous 10 years, having experienced a fairy-tale start-up with only 2 employees, my wife and I and exploding rapidly to almost 70 employees within that period.

We provide technical oil-field services to major oil and gas exploration companies and also to many independents. We pride ourselves as being a technologically innovative company operating in a niche market. Most of what we do revolves around fixing bad oil producing wells using sophisticated electronic tools, connected to computers and mechanical devices, which we installed into such wells. Our major competition comes from large multinational oil service companies.

We had experienced two tough back-to-back years and hit what appeared to be quagmire, a plateau of sorts, in our revenue growth.

Our operating statistics had started to unravel as we tried to meet the disparaging needs of our various clients. Resources were stretched, internal inertia required to get even the basic things done, was grinding and frustrating and employee morale was sagging. We kept experiencing unexplainable service-quality problems, yet everyone appeared to be working as hard as they possibly could. We had burnout and one of our key support staff even asked to resign her job, "to be home with baby".

We spent several months searching for solutions. We ordered stacks of books on quality management, I went to business school for an executive management program, and we hired consultants to develop a do-it-yourself approach to fixing the problem.

One morning, after receiving another client complaint, I typed the word "quality" in my Internet browser, to search for a quality program we could adapt to our unique situation. I ran into Bruce Snell's book-"Breaking the 4 barriers to quality". I ordered it while attending an executive management program at the Harvard business school.

I was intrigued after reading the book. The approach was a refreshing mixture of intuition and common sense. Yet it all fit together as a strategic and cohesive approach to the QUALITY solution.

After reading the book and getting other managers in our organization to read it, we decided to contact the BSG organization, to find out if they had any training courses or a program we could adapt to the rest of the organization.

I located a phone number from the website and called Bruce Snell.

It might sound like an unlikely story, but when we called Bruce, at the same time, he was also asking God to send him his first Internet client.

We connected immediately and found to our pleasure that we shared the same faith and belief in God. This was the beginning of a friendship and business relationship between Bruce and Karen and our family and company that has now spanned over 6 years.

Bruce immediately offered to travel from his location in California at the time, across the oceans, to train our company in the tenets of the four barriers.

Over the next few years, Bruce visited Nigeria several times and spent many days and nights working with our associates in Oildata. We dealt with breaking down the "4 barriers", developing our processes and procedures and gradually transforming our company into a dynamic and successful organization.

We developed the **Q-66** process together with all our associates and this exercise galvanized our staff and transformed our service quality, proving beyond doubt that indeed, quality has no borders.

At first, it was a major challenge getting the program started, because it was not obvious where to begin to solve the many problems that kept popping up. Our clients were losing patience with reoccurring failures, there were errors in reports, lack of follow up with ordering spares, missing invoices, missed appointments, cash-burn with accounts, poor maintenance problems, hours spent trying to locate documents etc.

It was against this context that we set about overcoming the first of the four quality barriers, "Fear". Fear generated inertia and enhanced the "blame culture" within the organization. It tapped into the level of mistrust among our staff, a situation that was borne out of the many quick-fix programs we had tried unsuccessfully to introduce. I remember the first round-table meeting with our people when we introduced the BaseWork Systems 2000 quality program. There was no single question from the audience when we opened the floor for questions after the many presentations on the subject.

We discovered that the greatest tool for breaking down this barrier was the "bottoms-up" participation of the various BaseWork Centers – Getting everyone involved in the process; from drivers to secretaries, managers and field-operators. Together with Bruce Snell, we identified the many "low hanging fruit" and set about learning, identifying and defining our procedures and processes. This process built confidence in our "associates" and their hands-on participation helped to develop "buy-in" and ownership of the program.

Breaking through barrier #2, "Lack of Written Communication" at our organization was analogous to breaking a habit or learning a new language. At most transitioning and innovation driven companies such as ours, we tended to pride ourselves as good communicators, having a hands-on, and get-it-done-right-away approach to solving problems. Unfortunately, most orders and internal requests tended to be verbal, easily forgotten or misunderstood, and worse still, the existing system lacked integrity and could not be held accountable. The net result was a lot of rework, frustrated and overworked employees and internal company inertia, with tons of paperwork and forms to fill out for basic requests, and off course the proverbial "firefighting".

Our steering committee, worked with the various BaseWork Centers to set up an order-request system to process all client and internal requests throughout the organization. We called it **FAST** and implemented the system around an online asset management system, using the order-request procedures we learned in the BSG training classes. The impact was immediate. We cut down the number of forms required to order materials and supplies and ship them to our field crews from 17 to 2.

We could now track and drill-down requests by the BaseWork Center. Folks in accounts, who usually got blamed for many missed deadlines, could now hold the rest of the organization accountable. The greatest benefit to the organization was in planning and budgeting. Every division now submits and updates their weekly monthly and bi-monthly requests ahead of time and managers are able to prioritize in advance rather than "on-the-fly", with an upset client at the other end of the phone.

Breaking down the quality barrier #3, "Lack of Written Procedure", was at the core of defining our growth and strategy for the next level in our organization. During the several one-on-one sessions with various BaseWork Centers, we quickly discovered that different work-groups or cells as we refer to them, executed client orders differently. There was a lot of improvising going on and we had come to depend on a few "gurus", whose expertise was neither written nor consistent.

Working with BSG, we collated our steps and procedures and connected our systems together. What emerged was a sixty-six-step process, which we christened the "**Q-66**" process. **Q-66** tied together our service delivery process from the first contact with the client, through the actual execution of the service, to a close-out review by management. This set up improvements and through learnings from the service delivery cycle, impacted the bottom line positively.

The process allowed all our associates, the technical sales engineers, field technicians and engineers, support and maintenance staff and managers to understand, visualize and participate in the big picture. As the Japanese say, we connected the "Gemba" or the core of our service delivery process to delivering value to our clients, while eliminating unnecessary repetitions and complete omissions.

Breaking through the fourth barrier, "Lack of training", created a company wide movement to develop data entry skills and disseminate a fundamental understanding of the process of quality and quality improvement. The most important learning benefit of the 24-month program was the commitment every associate (I guess you have picked up by now that all our employees are called associates.), to the monthly hour-long training meeting of every BaseWork Center involved in the program.

Showing up on time and timeliness at meetings was the greatest challenge and at the end, was one of the greatest benefits of the quality program at our company. We have expanded the foundational quality program to include on-the-job skills training; formal career based mentoring, competency mapping and certification for all our associates. We have created benchmarks and measures for monitoring and tracking progress across the company.

The benefits of the quality program at Oildata can be seen from the year-on-year results of one of our most important measures since the program was introduced. The average Job Quality Rating **JQR** (Best is 100% and worst is 0 %), which measures the quality of service delivery to our clients, has consistently grown from about 55% in 2006, to over 70% by the end of 2008. This measure includes data from independent client evaluations, Q-66 job-preparation and execution indices and maintenance-efficiency scores.

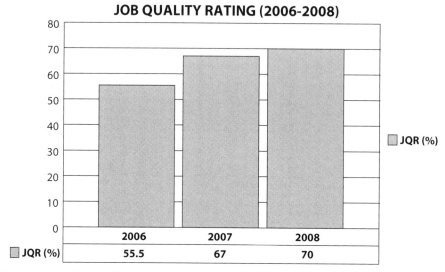

JOB QUALITY RATING (2006-2008)

JQR (%)	2006	2007	2008
JQR (%)	55.5	67	70

Figure 1.0: Job Quality Rating Statistics at Oildata (2006 – 2008)

We picked up a few lessons on the road to quality at our organization (We are still on that road!).

The first lesson was that quality transcends cultural and national boundaries. The "4 barriers" were prevalent at our company, similar to the many examples that Bruce highlights in his book. Knocking down these barriers involved applying the same tested principles of top-down management commitment and bottoms-up participation of every one in the organization. There were no short cuts.

We also discovered that commitment by senior management is critical in successfully pushing through major organizational change. We had a number of false starts, particularly with the folks involved in our field services. So, we never gave up, even when fire fighting got in the way and the program took a back seat.

One other important element in implementing the quality program at our company was the rub-off effect from the 24-month training program.

We slowly developed company-wide habits of punctuality, discipline, and record keeping, planning and holding each other accountable.

The classes helped us refocus on getting the job done right the first time and galvanized the whole organization around a common purpose.

It became apparent to most folks in the company that although most of the ideas presented in the "4-Barriers" appeared simple and intuitive, "common sense" was not quite so common when it came to implementation and follow through. Every new project threw up fresh challenges and sometimes sent us right back to "fire-fighting" mode.

We discovered that organizational change takes time and involves the active engagement of the entire organization for up to 24 months. This change process inevitably retained its dynamic nature, for it continues to challenge and transform our company today.

BaseWork Systems and the *4 barriers* address the softer human perspective of quality within an organization. Most quality improvement methods we came across often-emphasized rules and procedures, which tended to alienate the shop floor.

One of the first lessons we learn in the program are the base values, which happen to be the most abiding;

— Do what is morally and ethically correct
— Treat everyone as you want to be treated

Base values capture the core essence of our value-preposition;

Quality is an attitude and a journey worth taking for every individual and the organizations we work for - the impact goes beyond the bottom line.

There is a saying in Africa that **"the best time to plant a tree was twenty years ago, but the next best time is now."**

This word is used 4 times. I hope everyone knew what this meant and didn't need to use a dictionary like me.

Inertia - inertness, esp. with regard to effort, motion, action, and the like; inactivity; sluggishness.

A Positive Note

The only way you can continually improve the organization is to first define "how you are doing business."

By defining your systems you are improving them.

Once employees have defined their "BaseWork Centers", linking the processes together will start defining the organizations' systems.

The stage is now set for continuously improving the business.

Bruce

Introduction

Do you ever say to yourself, "I wonder where I'd be now, if I hadn't gone to college, or where I'd be if I had moved to Maine, or where I'd be if I hadn't married the girl of my dreams?" Sometimes I ask myself where I'd be, if I had never met Mike Smith.

My personal quest for a system of integrating quality into a company started by accident—the way most good things start.

Quality, for me, started through a business venture with Mike Smith in Santa Ana, California. Mike and I became friends and kept in contact on a fairly regular basis.

During that time, the economy in California peaked and started a downward spiral. Finally, in the late 80's and early 90's, it leveled out into a solid recession.

Unbeknown to me, the recession was assaulting my good friend, Mike. His business was spiraling downward with California's economy. Mike was in trouble!

Mike had a small company where he employed one hundred and twenty employees and fifteen salesmen. Because I was a very successful salesman at the time, he asked me if I would take a look at his business to see if there was anything I could do.

My first chore was to take a thorough look at his business. That sounds a whole lot easier than it actually was; it took an endless toll on my time. I did it, though, and to say I was shocked is an understatement. My friend Mike's company was in trouble. His sales had gone down from approximately $25 million to a dismal $13 million, and he was just about out of business.

Mike's situation, however, was typical. He had been following a path blazed by many companies which had experienced good sales growth. Company sales had been growing 10 to 15% annually, and Mike—like others with inefficiencies brought on by rapid growth was throwing bodies and money at the problems.

All good things end though and sales were no different—they peaked. Guess what happened? You're right. The problems of rapid growth were still there, but cash flow wasn't (the cash flow could no longer cover the inefficiencies). All of a sudden, Mike found himself with a tremendous overhead, a cash flow crunch, and a brand new facility to support (I forgot to tell you about the new building).

Since feeling sorry for ourselves was not a viable solution, Mike and I sat down to analyze the data garnered from my investigation. I pointed out that sales were not the only problem area. As a matter-of-fact, he had good salesmen. They seemed to be knowledgeable and had their fingers on the pulse of the industry. No, Mike's problems ran much deeper.

In addition to sales problems, the market had exhibited an overall decrease and gross profits had plummeted dramatically over the past three years. The result—business was out of control; throat cutting was the order of the day.

After working with the salesmen, I discovered that they were having all kinds of trouble. First, there was the price of the product Then the purchase orders weren't processed correctly, the billing wasn't done right, and they were having problems tracing the status of the product once they went into production. They also promised customers a five-day turnaround and were not meeting it.

Manufacturing, here I come! I now knew that sales were just the head of this evil serpent. So, I jumped into manufacturing with both of my (really big) feet. I needed more information. My discovery process uncovered problems with incomplete paperwork. The accountants had to run down salesmen to query the status of an account, as well as get instructions for proceeding with a particular contract.

My next quest for knowledge took me to the billing department where I discovered the paperwork was not correct. Billing was having trouble processing their work and getting it out on time.

To my horror, I had unearthed a total breakdown of the entire system. The breakdown and dysfunction of this business was not just sales but was to be found in almost every department. It was obvious that the whole company needed an overhaul.

After much discussion, Mike suggested we start a quality program. I agreed, but asked the question, "How?" Mike's friend had a quality program and suggested we meet with him and see if we couldn't use his program, or at least get some ideas so we would have a starting point.

That began my introduction to Dr. Deming, the father of modern TQM philosophy. I read everything he had written. I tried to get inside his head and understand his thoughts. This was a man that went to Japan in the 50's, when they had a negative net-worth, and helped them rebuild their economy around his concept of quality. His system was one of proven worth.

Obviously, we couldn't bring in Dr. Deming to solve Mike's problems, so my goal became the creation of a program that any business could afford to implement. Mike's business was just like all the other businesses out there. It needed a quality program, but couldn't afford to implement one (the available canned quality programs were just too expensive and not user friendly).

Now, all this ole-country-boy from Alabama (that's me) had to do was develop a good, inexpensive quality program that worked.

No big deal! I stepped back and asked, "what would this quality/ training program look like?"

The goal was to develop a formal training program with a structured format and defined curriculum while working within the quality concept. The program must be one that could be managed, monitored and the people held accountable. It must promote continuous improvement and start with the end in mind.

As I moved through different companies, I saw similarities with each company. Although each company believed that their problems were unique, all their problems fell into one of the four barriers to quality. I found the following problems:

1. Employees capabilities outgrew their positions.
2. There were problems as a company's leadership/ownership changed.
3. Existing training programs were not working.
4. There was a problem with quality even though the company was quality certified.
5. Profits were declining.
6. They out-grow their capabilities.

During the next seven years and 20,000 hours-on-the-job development, BaseWork Systems 2000 was created. Its modules were written and rewritten a "gazillion times". Its purpose is to integrate quality into every process, procedure and system in the company.

It contains a step-by-step process that was manageable, monitorable and held people accountable for quality.

Because of the holistic approach to quality, everyone in the company participates in the program and holds each other accountable for quality. By so doing, this encourages employees to grow personally and professionally through BaseWork Centers.

The whole person is held accountable for quality issues both personally and professionally. It is a true blending of people and process development led by strong management commitment. Impeccable business ethics is the foundation of the system.

Breaking Through the 4 Barriers to Quality is about the development of BaseWork Systems 2000. It contains stories and actual events of the workplace. Many of you will relate to the scenarios in the stories.

We are asking you to step back and look at the problems within your organization. Look at the problems without pointing fingers of blame at managers or co-workers. The problems are not because of people but because of the four barriers to quality. Please understand that 99% of all employees want to do a good job—it's the four barriers that prevent that from happening.

BaseWork Systems 2000 is destined to become the foundation of all future training programs. This book will not sit on the shelf. It will be used as a reference on your day-to-day experience with making your organization a quality organization. Enjoy the awareness!

Bruce

WHAT ARE THE 4 BARRIERS TO QUALITY

I thought I'd satisfy your curiosity immediately by telling you what the four barriers are and discussing them briefly. Be forewarned, however! After reading these chapters, you will understand the four barriers, but you'll need to read the rest of the book to learn how to eliminate them in your company. That's not much to ask of you—in return for a workable, productive quality program in your company—is it?

98% of the problems encountered by an organization in building business infrastructure fall into the following four barriers to quality:

1. **Fear of expression and/or actions.**
2. **Lack of communication (verbal and/or written).**
3. **Lack of written procedure.**
4. **Lack of training.**

If the four barriers are faced by using the BaseValues- concept, quality can be achieved.

BaseValues:The foundation of principles and rules that determines conduct and habit, which in turn affect all employees' common welfare. The company must hold and be held accountable for these BaseValues. The underlying structure is built on "the two rules":

1. Do what is morally and ethically correct.
2. Treat everyone as you want to be treated.

PART I

As I moved through different companies, I saw the same problems appearing in the same fashion. Ninety-eight percent of a company's problems fall into the four barriers to quality. The remaining two percent are due to external influences such as the economy, competition and government regulations. The funny thing is that each company believed their problem to be unique.

Over the years, we discovered that while each barrier was unique they were related to each other. Because of their interrelated nature, one problem-area could not be resolved without improving the other problem-areas. We also discovered that the sequence of the barriers contributed to their resolution. For example: fear caused lack of communication, which caused lack of procedures, which caused lack of training. Addressing the four barriers to quality in the proper sequence contributes to the transition of a quality-oriented company.

In order for your company to address the FEAR, there must be a motivation to change the way you do business. This change has its impetus in the leadership of the company. Effective communication creates a team atmosphere conducive to solving problems.

When employees communicate without fear of reprisal, written procedures can be prepared. The employee doing the specific job must devise the procedures. Other employees involved in the task devise the procedures that relate to them. Written procedures provide the tool for training. Training must be job specific and contain a formal training program that includes cross training.

I firmly believe that most employees want to do a good job, but are stopped by the four barriers. These barriers prevent employees from growing and taking pride in their work. Their commitment to the company grows as the four barriers are removed.

1
BREAKING THROUGH FEAR

THE FACE OF FEAR

The first barrier to quality is fear: fear of expression or action. If you are not making a decision because you fear what could happen, that is fear of action. Fear of expression is when you do not communicate your thoughts because of fear of what could happen. Maybe the last time you shared your thoughts it fell on deaf ears, or got you ridiculed and made fun of.

Let's look into the face of fear and its many manifestations in the workplace.

The Open-Door Policy

Almost every organization I visit says it has an open-door policy, but doesn't really. The CEO tells everyone he has one because he sincerely wants it and believes he has it. An employee wanting to take advantage of the open-door policy just doesn't do it. It is a pre-conceived open-door policy. The CEO will never get input, even though he claims to have a policy allowing employees to walk up anytime and talk about anything. In reality, they can't. The frustrating thing I see for most CEO's is when a problem explodes. They sit down frustrated with the person involved and ask why they weren't informed. The company's informal structure and the employee's fear keep that from happening.

The Fear of Expression

Maybe we feel we have a better way of doing something. We may want to correct something, or we may just want to address an issue that is not right. The fear of expression keeps that from happening.

For example, the fear of expression could be the boss coming to you with a problem in your department. You know what the problem is and you know what the answer is. You are asked by your boss why something is going out late. You know the answer and the solution, but you know as soon as you walk out the door, you'll be in trouble because you spoke up. That's fear of expression. It can go as far as an employee simply shutting down and just agreeing with whatever is being said.

The Fear of Action

An example of fear of action is the employee who was responsible for manufacturing. Before leaving for the evening, the Vice President of Manufacturing told the night manager to get the product out immediately at all cost. The Vice President didn't communicate with anyone else in manufacturing that same sense of urgency.

Due to a down-sizing initiative, the production employees who had been laid off were the ones responsible for putting the instructional labels on the product. In this situation, production has been ordered to get the product out, and 99% was done.

What about applying the labels; who's going to do that? Someone simply placed the labels in the box. They didn't put them on the product as required.

The product was sent out that way. Short term, they met production and quota. The fear of action (not taking time to apply the labels) caused the product to go out without the labels applied correctly.

You can justify all day that the labels really don't mean anything, but that's not quality. What you'll find out is that if the defected product or service is passed on to your internal customer and sent back to you—the cost of that product/service has just doubled. Each time the defective product/service makes it to another BaseWork Center, then the cost is doubled again! By the time the customer finds the defect at their place of business, the cost may have been increased by as much as 100 times.

When we look at the issue, we can say the label doesn't mean anything and the customer will know to read the manual before using the product. Believe me, that is not the way to do business. You can justify anything, but fear of action means that we don't do something that's right, because in this case, the Vice President will get all over us when we don't meet the deadline.

Holding Each Other Accountable

Usually, you'll find very little accountability internally because no one owns the process. No one is given responsibility for anything except when it is a responsibility of convenience. That means you're responsible now because I don't have time to deal with it.

What happens is that no one will hold anyone accountable for quality because people are afraid someone will come back and attack them. If something goes wrong, they won't hold quality responsible. They'll just pass it on and nod to agree on whatever the situation is. There is no accountability there. When there is fear, no one will step up and be accountable because there is no system in place for accountability.

Hidden Agendas

People who won't allow you to know the real reasons for their actions have hidden agendas. Most grow from fear, fear of losing their job or fear of being passed over for promotion. Remove the fear and you remove the motivation for hidden agendas.

Double Standards

Double standards exist in the environment of fear because the procedure is not being monitored. For example, the boss will let one employee not show up on time but punishes another for the same offense—that's a double standard. Management uses a policy and enforces it only when convenient. That usually happens when there is fear associated for some reason. The policies are used to get at an employee rather than to do what is right. Double standards frustrate so much because one person is held accountable and the other person isn't.

Holding Hostage

Holding Hostage Employees

I often talk about ruling a company through fear. The concept of holding hostage means fear through coercion.

One of the things I often hear is that the employees are saying such things as, "I don't like what's going on, but if you fire me or give me another job, I'll file a stress claim."

Or, "If you don't let me work a particular job or a certain shift, I'm going to quit, and I'll file a stress claim." This is what I call employees holding a company hostage.

Holding Hostage The Management

The management will use the same kind of leverage. "If you don't like it, I'll (the manager) leave and I'm the only one who holds this place together because your employees don't care. I'm the best thing that has ever happened to this company." That's management holding the company hostage.

Holding Hostage The Company

Companies can hold employees hostage, also. The greatest example is, "If you don't like it, leave." That kind of attitude doesn't resolve any issue and only frustrates the employees.

Usually the person involved in the "hostage situation", whether it is employee, management, or the company, has a lot of knowledge about his job and refuses to share it with anyone else (fear). When the quality program is implemented, they resist giving up the information necessary for transitioning the company to quality.

There can be a lot of reasons for this. Usually the employee will talk about why you have to keep him on payroll. The hostage part comes when he threatens to reveal skeletons in the closet or reveal situations where the company did something wrong to a customer.

These types of things hold a company hostage. Once you start giving in to these situations, employees will use many things as leverage. That will stifle the growth of the company.

Change is Fearful

Most organizations are in constant change because most companies are informal. That creates an environment of fear. When you're looking at trying to change from informal to a structured or formal organization—whatever change there is, no matter how great or small—fear is the outcome.

Change internally has to be manageable. People have to know where they need to start and where they're going. It should be well thought out, planned, and monitored. Change should begin with an end in sight. The reason for change must be reinforced daily with all employees. There can never be change with hidden agendas.

Insecurity

When an employee doesn't feel secure in his job, he will not commit to making decisions or improvements. If you just laid ten people off, he will fear he's next.

If an employee doesn't know where the company is going, she won't be secure in her job. Instead of getting settled in and getting involved in the job, she stands back trying to figure out what the next day will bring, or whether she will have a job tomorrow—all the while trying to deal with her insecure feelings. Companies must positively reinforce security for the employees. What is feared most is losing one's job. The goal must be to maintain the employee's job and build the company.

Churning Leadership

Many top managers leave an organization in one to three years (churning leadership). The good manager that has tried to do what is right and has learned her job well gets bogged down internally within the department or division because of change.

The constant turnover in management presents an inconsistency in leadership and management. The employees are trying to figure out what the new standard operating procedure will be.

I have talked with several companies about changing leadership. Every time they get a new manager their whole philosophy of business changes. Not having direction, planning, and long-term commitment, agreed to by management, causes turnover in management. The manager may see that there is nowhere else to go because of the informal structure of the organization.

Oftentimes, we churn leadership because we need new blood to implement changes and budget cuts. The manager hits her goals, gets her bonus, and then moves on. The churning cycle starts over again.

Churning Employees

Many employees also stay with a company only one to two years before leaving. If you are having constant employee turnover, a common complaint is, "We don't want to train them because they leave." My question is, why are they leaving? If we're training them so well, why would they want to leave?

The good employee in an informal organization is constantly beating his head against a wall. The first thing a company loses is the good employees. They can always find a job, but the bad employee will stay on as long as he can. Be aware of churning employees. Many times we don't have long-term commitment to our employees. We put them in a spot and there is no way to improve themselves. If they speak up, they're out of there.

Informal Corporate Structure

The last time some companies sat down and drew up an organizational chart was years ago. What has happened during the interim to jobs and employees? They never really formalized the way they were doing business, so they have an informal structure. Some people are held accountable and some are not.

The fear is that they will never step up to address the informal corporate structure because they're afraid that they'll make someone mad. If employees have to define what they're doing, then management is going to define what they're doing. That is what happens when the product of fear is the informal corporate structure.

Power Structure: Manipulated

When you have fear in an organization, an informal power structure can emerge, with the power being manipulated by a few people. Even though the CEO feels she still has the same existing structure as in the beginning, she doesn't. The company is really managed by the informal power structures that are wreaking havoc while constructing their own departmental kingdoms.

Departmental Walls and Job Division

When there is fear in an organization, one department or division doesn't talk to the other because literally, their directions and goals are going in different ways and they have different agendas.

For example, the last time an employee spoke up about another department, he got in trouble, or they slowed up his paperwork to get even with him. Departments build walls and job division between employees, internal customers and suppliers. Because of fear, employees don't speak up and handle the issues. They all accept the status quo instead of having the vehicle to handle what is right.

Mental and Physical Intimidation

You think you've grown beyond the bully in the school yard, but there are people at work who bully others internally. Believe me, it does happen. There are guys that push their weight, height, size, status, or job title around.

Negative employees are constantly intimidating other employees by suggesting they do terrible work, making insulting remarks, or insinuating they are lucky to even have a job. There is physical and mental intimidation in a company. Watch the one percent unsatisfactory employees—they have learned to master this.

Mental intimidation can be sitting in the boardroom when the boss asks for input. If the employee doesn't say what the boss wants to hear, the boss beats that employee into submission. After several hours, the boss gets what he wants, and everyone leaves and does what they wanted to do in the first place. After all, no one is being held accountable. Mental intimidation beats the life out of your organization.

Unhappy Employees

This is a huge cost to a company. Fear is frustrating, because it hits in many different ways and involves different things employees do daily on the job. It even affects employees' home life.

If you ask why employees are unhappy, one answer is because of inconsistency. They are held accountable sometimes and other times not. There are double standards and hidden agendas. Their peers are being spiteful or hateful to them.

The fear of these things causes them to withdraw from positive participation and they become very unhappy about their jobs. Once this begins, it is very difficult to turn around, because an unhappy employee is an unproductive employee.

TOUGH DECISIONS

Story #1

When we begin the program, we ask the CEO to sign off on our checklist for success. The list has twenty-two items regarding the way we are going to conduct and do business (the company's Base Values). It also deals with our two rules: 1) do what is morally and ethically correct, and 2) treat everybody as you want to be treated. At the bottom of the check list for success is the statement, **MAKE TOUGH DECISIONS.**

This means that the CEO is going to have to make tough decisions about employees. Statistically, one percent of employees will remove themselves from the program and five percent will resist the program from time to time. Usually, we will see the funnel down effect where one percent of the workforce will leave.

When we talk about tough decisions, we don't necessarily mean that a tough decision is firing somebody. A tough decision is holding somebody accountable. For example, we have a manager that violates one of the rules of the company. The CEO is going to have to back the program and the employees in regard to that particular quality issue.

Many of these tough decisions have to do with the sales force. We talked earlier about a company being held hostage by an employee. The salesman knows that the procedure requires them to complete the Purchase Order. Ultimately, a salesman will test the system. When that top producing salesman refuses to follow procedure, the CEO must hold him accountable.

The CEO says, "This is the procedure. Everyone agreed on it and you're putting me in an awkward position. I'm doing it and everyone in the program is doing it. Your boss is doing it. Please tell me why you're different." When the CEO presents it that way, the person will follow through. If the salesman has not been taught the procedure, the coordinator will be involved in handling that particular quality issue or conflict.

So, when we say tough decisions, we mean tough decisions. Everyone must be held accountable if we are to avoid double standards and hidden agendas. If you let somebody slide in the program, it sets the tone. People begin to think that this is business as usual with the double standards and hidden agendas. If the other guy doesn't have to do it, then why do I? Our last resort is to fire somebody, probably the toughest decision of all. We haven't had to do that yet. One thing is for sure, though. Tough decisions boil down to holding everybody, from top management to the day laborer, accountable.

> #1 *When dealing with tough decisions, deal only with data and not emotion.*

HOW DO WE ADDRESS THE FEAR?

Hopefully, you now agree with me that fear exists in the workplace. Now, the question remaining unanswered is how to deal with it. How can workplace fear be resolved? I propose the elimination of fear through a seven step process.

1. Letter of Commitment by the President/CEO

The quality program needs a letter of commitment written by the president/CEO of the company stating that he is 100% behind the quality program, that he is committed both short and long term to the program, and that the program has the total support of the owner and/or the Board of Directors. It must be a strongly written letter supporting long-term commitment of the program. Dr. Deming was able to turn Japan's economy around in 3-5 years (now that's commitment).

2. BaseValues

In the letter, there must be a commitment in writing of the organization's BaseValues. These BaseValues are the organization's intrinsic social principles, goals and values held accountable and accepted by the company. They include the two rules: 1) do what is morally and ethically correct, and 2) treat everybody as you want to be treated. When in conflict, the conflict is a quality issue and all quality issues will be handled by the coordinator in training. They have to be firm. The only way the organizational change will happen is by management putting it in writing—walking the walk, and talking the talk.

3. Quality Issues

There will be problems in the organization regarding conflict between the two rules. The two rules can either impact process, procedure, policy, or emotions—it doesn't matter. The program has a written process that will handle all quality issues. Quality issues are signed or unsigned statements of inconsistency. The goal is not to pin blame, but to bring solution. The only way that will be accomplished is by holding responsible parties accountable.

HOW TO ADDRESS
PERSONAL CONFLICT

Story #2

A personal quality issue occurs when we are in conflict with either our BaseValues or our two rules. These two rules are: 1) do what is morally and ethically correct, and 2) treat everybody as you want to be treated. In my program we don't particularly care who said what, or why. We are not trying to pin the blame anywhere. Our goal is to resolve the issue.

Every organization must have BaseValues. Our position is: if an employee feels it's a problem, we must address it regardless of our own personal opinion. If we demonstrate a tendency to write issues off as not really being problems, soon employees will stop bringing issues up. Quality issues must be addressed by sitting down and focusing on both sides of the issue. We encourage each person to look at the issue from the other's standpoint.

When employees are being held accountable for a particular quality issue, it usually stops. Many people say and do things that they don't believe are wrong. Others, however, see things differently. Even though the first person didn't do anything deliberately, someone else may take it as being wrong because it affected their environment and department. The person who perceives it incorrectly must have an avenue to address the issues.

> #2 *The focus of addressing a quality issue is not in pinning the blame, but in coming to an agreement/solution.*

4. Probus Leadership

Probus is a Latin word for honesty and integrity. All management activities must be conducted with these principles in mind. Probus Leadership *is* honesty and commitment.

5. Walk the Walk and Talk the Talk

When the company talks about long- or short-term commitment by the owners and management of the company, about doing what is morally and ethically correct, and about treating everybody as you want to be treated, management must lead by example. The employees will only participate if the guy signing the check has committed to the program. It is very important that the leadership lead by example; they must walk the walk and talk the talk because without management buy-in, it's not going to happen.

6. Quality Will Create New Jobs

Quality will not cost jobs, but it will create new jobs. You have to be patient with the quality program. It doesn't happen over night. Fifty years of data exist to support that quality lowers the cost of doing business, which in turn, lowers costs to consumers. That in turn, generates more customers and more jobs. You have to believe that quality will work. It takes time and must be reinforced day in and day out.

7. The Belief in the Commitment to Quality

You must have a commitment to quality, but at the same time have the understanding that it will take time to achieve. You must put it in writing that quality is a day-to-day process of going from non-structured to structured, from the current way of doing business to a quality way of doing business. You must be patient and communicate what you're doing day in and day out to all employees.

THE TWO RULES

Story #3

Before we take my program into an organization, we have the CEO sign off on what we call our two rules. These rules are a part of BaseValues or ethics of that organization. The rules are: 1) do what is morally and ethically correct, and 2) treat everybody as you want to be treated. Conflict is a quality issue and the quality coordinators address all quality issues.

As we look at this, there are a lot of problems in companies that are not addressed in human resource policy or procedure. There are conflicts between employees and leadership or employees and employees. We worked at figuring out how we could put this in writing in an enforceable fashion and yet still have the support of the employees. There are so many different things that can go wrong in a company—you can't write a procedure for everything.

When going into a company, you may find a pamphlet in their lobby that gives the organization's mission statement and vision. I can guarantee you that this is absolutely meaningless to 99% of the organization. Usually what happens is the Board of Directors makes this statement up and they really believe it. They post it in the lobby and want all employees to go out and implement it. But that's about as far as it goes. They are not walking the walk. They're talking it, but they aren't putting it into play.

The two rules came into being because of an incident that happened when we were infrastructuring a company. One of the employees attended a meeting and then got scolded by his superintendent for not being on the production line. The employee complained that we talked about quality, but that wasn't quality! I agreed.

To deal with this situation, we had to think about how we could attack these issues. The only way we found we could do that was to have the rules and hold everybody accountable. There cannot be any double standards. This includes management and supervisors. Leadership must set the tone of how they are doing business from both ethical and business perspectives. So, we have to develop the BaseValues and ethics of the company, come to an agreement on them, and hold everybody accountable for them. Once the employees see that everybody is held accountable, then there will be a change of attitude. Fear and the other barriers begin to disappear. We now have a way to handle much of the conflict in organizations.

Most companies that have a huge human resource department still don't have a way to handle such problems and personal conflicts. Because there is an absence of these two rules, they have no way for employees to settle interdepartmental conflicts. Left unattended, the conflicts blow up and become major problems.

> *#3* *The two rules are: 1) do what is morally and ethically correct, and 2) treat everybody as you want to be treated.*

SEE THE RESULTS

When you start removing the fear, you begin to see things happen. Below, I itemize seven things that regularly occur when fear is removed.

1. Consistency

The biggest thing that happens internally, once the program gets started, is consistency. Consistency is something many employees have never seen either in their work or home lives. Consistency is, in effect, being secure. Security promotes trust.

By being consistent, leadership shows good faith and the employee begins to trust the company.

2. Leadership

You move from being "managed" to a leadership form of business. The formal management structure no longer has to be a hard-line structure. In fact, you want to train everyone in the company to be a manager of his or her own BaseWork Center. That creates leadership. Management now has consistency and a tool for training. Instead of being dictatorial and telling people what to do; they can now lead the organization.

3. Trust

There is no end to what can happen when you promote trust in an organization. There is also no bigger asset to quality than trust.

4. Respect

Once you have trust, right behind it comes respect—not just with leadership, but leadership with employees, employees with unions, and unions with leadership. Once you remove all the personal issues, no one has hidden agendas. They're simply addressing the issues and solving the problems. It becomes an open book. Anyone can resolve a problem. You start to respect one another because you're now communicating and dealing daily without fear of action or expression.

You can figure out and see what each person is doing day in and day out, and see how important the other guy is, because you now understand his job. It becomes just as important as your job.

5. Ask Questions Openly and Honestly and Get Open and Honest Answers

The ultimate goal is to walk up to anyone in the organization and ask an open and honest question and get an open and honest answer. That goes for all employees from the floor sweeper to the CEO.

I often hear a CEO say she's busy and would rather delegate down. Remember, the main job of everyone in the company is to promote quality within the organization. In the beginning of the quality program, because of the frustrations of the four barriers, the CEO will have to spend time listening. If the CEO has to spend two hours a day for the next year just handling issues or listening and talking to her employees, believe me, she cannot invest her time or money more wisely.

My next observation is that if you all adhere to the two rules, there will be no finger-pointing. Sometimes you need to blow steam off your chest, and sometimes you need to know someone is listening. Remember, once you start removing the four barriers to quality, there are no hidden agendas or fear, and literally, you can talk to everyone. Before you blow up, you can handle the issues one on one, because you've learned how to do that, rather than let an issue fester to a point of conflict.

6. Secure with Leadership and Job

The biggest thing that happens is that you become secure with the leadership, management and your job.

You feel like you have job security, because you can trust management and each other. You're no longer beating up management.

7. Free Flow Of Information

Within most organizational structures, the arrows all point down. In my program, there is a diamond shape with arrows pointing in all directions. That means anyone in the company can give and receive information. There is no one-way direction in the organization. If communication needs to go all the way up to the top—that's the way it goes. That is truly a free flow of information. Once you remove the fear, you're free to flow information up and down the line.

CORPORATE SETS THE TONE

Story #4

The corporate office must set the tone for change in an organization. If a company says they are going to implement a quality program, the corporate office should become the jumping off point. As you build your model of what the company is going to do, you need to start with the corporate office. After all, who better knows what is expected of the organization? They are the ones who maintain contact with all the divisions and employees.

Corporate needs to figure out how the quality program is to be conducted and disseminate the plan to the divisions. The important thing to remember is that, from day one, the corporate office needs to project the culture regarding elimination of **the four barriers to quality**. They must adhere to the two rules: 1) do what is morally and ethically correct, and 2) treat everybody as you want to be treated—our BaseValues.

As we move forward with the program, corporate can emphasize its intent by the way they answer the phone, how they resolve issues, and how they talk about problems. Corporate is key in transitioning the way they change their business infrastructure.

Corporate must be the leader and the example of how they want their employees and divisions to act and interact. The employee cannot do it by themselves. The corporate office must set the tone and direction for them.

Corporate needs to change the concept that the only time they are heard from or seen is when they are telling somebody to do something (usually without input). A lot of times that is the only interaction with departments or divisions. Let's change that to where corporate is interacting with everybody. Let's move from a dictatorial style of management to one of partnership based on trust.

Let's give an example. Corporate is redoing the budget and has to cut 10% from the cost of doing business. We say expenses are out of control and we're losing money. What we usually do is send out a memo, or have a meeting saying the budget must be cut 10%. When we leave the meeting, no one has been given clear direction on how that should happen.

Now it's interpretation time! Each department must interpret what corporate wants, and then do the best they can. But it is only their interpretation. One might quit buying coffee every month. Another might lay off an employee. Another might quit servicing a particular program for its customers. Everybody is doing the best they can cutting 10% of the budget.

My program's position is that such an approach is unfair. Corporate needs to come in and say, "We need to cut 10%; how can we help you achieve that? What are the ways that you think we can cut 10%? You tell us what we should do." Please remember, corporate should be looked upon for support. Corporate's role needs to change from dictatorial to service. How can we help you? You tell us what you need. You tell us what we can do. How do we do it? Let me be there to support you. Let us use our assets to help you accomplish the goal we've given you. Let's improve the way we do business. It's unfair for corporate to make demands without support. They must provide the tools and direction. Let's move corporate from dictatorial to being respective, pro-active, listening and supportive. Corporate should not be feared, but instead, respected for how they can help. This is doable, so let's do it!

> #4 *Corporate needs to move from a dictatorial "do as I say" attitude to a more "how can I help you do your job" attitude. Corporate's main job should be to help its employees, divisions and companies do a better job.*

A Positive Note

"The 4 Barriers to Quality hinder the organization's personal, process and professional development"

Bruce

2

LACK OF COMMUNICATION: VERBAL AND/OR WRITTEN

In this chapter we will discuss the second of the four barriers to quality: lack of communication. First we will discuss the products of the lack of communication, then how we address it, and finally, its results. There are 15 products that result from the lack of communication. They are as follows:

1. Shut-Down Employees

An employee usually shuts down in an organization when he has no where to go with his thoughts, ideas, concerns, or requests. The lack of structure and the informal way of doing business in the organization has frustrated the employee. These shut-down employees can turn out to be some of your better employees because they have really tried at one time to step out, get involved, and make their work environment a better place. However, the lack of systems beats them into submission. These employees' problems are a direct product of lack of communication.

2. Misunderstanding of What is Expected

Misunderstanding can be from one work center to another. I call these internal suppliers/customers, people to whom you give and receive your work. A lot of times, once you get in and start defining your BaseWork Centers, processes, steps, and procedures, the problems go away. They were merely gaps between the BaseWork Centers. One person's understanding of what is expected or needed can be different from another's. By not having the information in writing, or possessing a formal procedure, misunderstandings often happen. They can result in not only poor quality, but a shut-down employee, as well as bad communication and hostility.

FLIP CHARTS

Story #5

One of my client's companies ordered some flip charts from an office supply company. When the flip charts arrived, they were in a very small box. To make them fit, the shipper had folded them in thirds. If you have ever used flip charts, you know the folding ruined them. They knew they couldn't use them so they called back and explained what had happened. The office supply company demonstrated great service and got them back in a day. Guess what happened? Whoever loaded the second order, did it the same way. The client then had two orders folded in thirds. The company finally sent somebody to pick up the flip charts.

This is a very simple example of non-quality—the type of mistakes that eat away at our customers. We aren't listening to them or thinking through quality. Let's look at the person who put the flip charts in the box. Believe me, she was probably trying to do the best she could, but more than likely never received feedback regarding the packing problem. That is an example of lack of feedback concerning a known quality issue which was never directed down to the point where correction must take place. Since the simplest things can aggravate our customers, we need to have everyone in the quality chain.

> #5 *Sometimes the simplest thing to your customer is the most frustrating.*

3. Employees Doing What They Perceive is Wanted

This happens time and time again. You go into a meeting and walk out with what you perceive your manager or customer wanted. You then go out and do it and guess what? What you thought, and what they thought, were two completely different things. What you've done is waste time, energy, effort and money, and you have built up a ton of frustration. All you're really trying to do is what you believe is right. When you don't have it in writing, then it is left to perception.

4. Frustration

One of the bigger things that happen when you have lack of communication is total frustration. You are being held accountable for one thing, one standard on a given day, and the next day it's completely different, or it is someone else's responsibility. That happens because of the inconsistency of policy, procedure, and product. It's a new day, everyday, and the standard for tomorrow is not necessarily the standard for today. Employees get frustrated because it's a no win situation.

5. Doing Things Over

Employees spend a lot of the workday doing things over. Why? Miscommunication or a complete absence of communication is the usual culprit.

6. No Communication

It can be very frustrating when an employee asks a question and is left waiting around for an answer. No communication can be as frustrating as miscommunication.

WHY CAN'T WE SHARE THE NUMBERS?

Story #6

One of the problems in the business world is that a lot of us really don't understand the cost of doing business. Because of this lack of understanding, many times employees make unrealistic demands on management. When management's answer is no, oftentimes it is a financial no.

The easiest way to understand the aforementioned problem is to give an example. Let's say we're at a location where a manager has 10 drivers. His drivers seem to be overworked and tired. Since the employees complain all the time about the workload, the manager approaches his supervisor with a request for another driver. What we really need to happen here is for the manager to look at the numbers. For example, he needs to understand and consider the cost of doing business. When he has that level of understanding, he knows that in order for us to hire another driver, we must increase revenue by 15%. If we increase our numbers, we can afford another driver. This makes the manager aware of the cost of doing business. It also helps to format goals regarding methods for achieving the additional 15% so we can hire the additional driver.

One of the first things we need to do is share the numbers with our employees (confidential numbers aside) and help them understand the cost of doing business. We need to make sure management understands the profit-loss statement. Our position is, if he doesn't understand the numbers, how can he effectively manage the day-to-day operation. We should have some base numbers and budget items that are examined and monitored monthly such as inventory, overtime, expenses, etc. In regard to our employees, we need to be honest and up-front when sharing the numbers. For example, if they believe they have a particular route that needs overtime to complete, the best way to deal with the issue is through data analysis. We need to sit down with that employee and show her the cost of doing business. Based on that route, we need x amount and, currently, we're 35% below that figure. In order to get another person or split the route, we need to increase the volume of business.

When everyone understands the numbers, we all have parameters and goals within which we can work. Remember, we all have to be honest. We cannot inflate or deflate the numbers depending on the particular issue. We have to abide by the two rules 1) do what is morally and ethically correct, and 2) treat everybody as you want to be treated.

I have discovered that with most employees, they know they will receive their paycheck regardless of mistakes made. If the employee understands the numbers, he will understand that those mistakes cost the company money. Every time we send another truck or employee out, it is costing us money. We should be able to give them very specific information regarding operating expenses. Let's say it cost 64 dollars an hour to send the truck out and the employee adds another 10 dollars; now they can understand the cost of mistakes.

The issue is for the employee to understand that every time they do something that is not in their BaseWork Center or make an error such as double work, redundant work, or missing a shipping order, it costs us money. If the delivery person is spending 10% to 15% of his time taking back inventory, then that's costing us 15%. The only way we can get employees to understand this is to train them regarding numbers and the cost of doing business.

That brings us to quotas. I don't recommend rewarding quotas. Yes, you have to have targets for monitoring the cost of doing business, but my belief is that incentive programs get blown out of proportion. If we're not careful, we end up spending 90% of our time trying to figure out how we can get our bonus, who gets a bonus, and discussing the fairness of the system. We forget our mission to service customers.

Another problem I face while trying to bring change to a company is a defensiveness and lack of trust based on the four barriers to quality. Employees oftentimes think the company merely wants to squeeze more profit out of them. Consequently, they want to know what is in it for them. You need to have an answer to that question. A really good answer is "Long-term employment." That's a hard thing for employees, no matter how disgruntled they are, to dispute. I have seen too many managers get backed into a corner trying to justify change. They get defensive when asked to answer the employees' "what's in it for me" question. We don't need to make it a personal issue; we just need to emphasize long-term employment and stress that the company needs to make money in order for that to happen. As we talk about managing and monitoring through the use of data, BaseWork Centers should step back and look at the way they are doing business from a cost and expense basis. We want everyone managing their own BaseWork Centers with the data given and available to them.

#6 *A procedure is only good when it is held accountable. Everyone in the organization should understand break-even analysis and the cost of doing business in their particular BaseWork Center. Only then can we make informed decisions based on data.*

---

7. No One To Talk To About Their Concerns

When they have little or no communication, employees don't even know how to talk to one another. They have little practice expressing their concerns or resolving difference. That, of course, has a lot to do with their lack of interpersonal skills. Concerns are put in the form of negative rap instead of learning how to address particular issues at work. When you have no one to talk to about your concerns, it starts building up internally. You start to think that everyone in the organization is out to hurt you. It compounds and builds and one day you explode. Also, you may feel you don't have anyone to talk to in relation to your personal life. You don't have the skills to talk to someone at home, much less someone with whom you work. You've become shut-down, lonely, and isolated because you don't have the skills to communicate with others. You become a steaming pot waiting to boil.

8. Feeling Alone

Many times your employees feel like they are the only ones in the company that care. They work hard to be at work on time every day, to make a better product, and to help your customers. They may feel that they are the only ones who really want to get the job out and do what the company wants.   Because of the lack of verbal or written communication, they feel like they are alone and they're carrying a huge load all by themselves.

9. Inconsistency

Verbal communication is very negatively impacted by implied procedure or anything not written. There is a terrible inconsistency with the process, policy and procedure. One day it's acceptable and the next day it isn't—depending on who's interpreting that particular process or procedure. There are great inconsistencies from what you presume is wanted, what is actually needed, and what you're doing.

10. Negative Rap

Most employees have learned at least one way to communicate informally, especially in an organization where most don't have good communication skills. Their acquired skill is in the negative arena. I call that negative rap. For example, a fellow employee says, "Hey, you look awful this morning." My reply is, "You look worse than I do." The banter turns into a conversation of negative rap, which seems to have no end. It is very contagious and a lot of conflict comes from this.

Some people say they've always communicated like that and they're just good friends. The problem with that is it registers mentally in our minds and emotions as a negative and our minds can't separate the two. I don't care if two guys have been friends forever; one will eventually have enough of the negative rap. When he's decided he's had enough and he won't take any more, conflict happens. That's why nothing positive is going to come from negative rap.

If the only way you can communicate is with something negative about someone, you don't need to communicate at all. That's not the answer. Communicate in a positive manner by learning the skills necessary to get your ideas and emotions across to others. Negative rap is a cancer that will eat away at the foundation of an organization.

HIDDEN AGENDA

Story #7

The program's definition of hidden agenda is: to keep from others, knowledge about the real reason for your response. Typically, a hidden agenda benefits the holder directly or indirectly at the expense of another.

There are endless and countless stories of hidden agendas, not only in our personal lives but in our business lives. It can be as simple as, "The reason you can't go to the seminar is because you've been complaining you're short-handed. So, how can you tell us you want to go to the seminar and take a day off, when, on the other hand, you are saying you are too understaffed? No, you can't go."

The hidden agenda is, "I'm really still angry that you suggested we need to hire additional employees," as opposed to addressing the issue saying, "No, you can't go because we can't afford it, or we just can't make the time." We turn around and try to make a point back to that person instead of simply telling the truth of the situation.

A hidden agenda could be "Sure, Bruce, go ahead and take Friday off." Maybe I say I really don't need to take the day off after all, but now they insist I take it off. The hidden agenda is that they have a friend who is out of work and they want to bring him in to work that day and pay him double time.

A lot of hidden agendas involve giving half the information to individuals or to departments. By so doing, you get what you want. The hidden agenda takes different forms (i.e. not enough information, too much information, or twisted or misdirected information or actions).

The only reason I'm being nice to you today is because later on this afternoon, I am going to ask you to do something that you wouldn't necessarily want to do. I'll be nice to you—making you feel guilty if you turn me down.

The use of a hidden agenda is manipulation. It is not doing what is right. Look again at the two rules: do what is morally and ethically correct, and treat everybody as you want to be treated. The hidden agenda is one reason for the development of the quality issue.

Hidden agendas are rampant in most organizations. It can be as simple as someone saying, "I didn't stop by to ask you if you wanted coffee because I was busy." Well, the real reason was he didn't ask because he didn't like the person.

Honesty and integrity are key ingredients of the organization's BaseValues. We have to let honesty flow freely by communicating and being concerned for one another, without intentionally hurting someone else's feelings.

So, how do we get rid of hidden agendas? We follow the two rules. We also hold everybody accountable. We learn to negotiate and communicate with our fellow employees. We don't take issues personally or make issues personal. We just learn to communicate and do so in writing.

That one percent of employees that are unproductive will remove themselves from the situation. A lot of times hidden agendas are not as much an issue of not giving information as they are of people protecting themselves. If I give them this, they're going to hurt me. People learn not to trust fellow employees.

Most programs out there totally fail because they don't have a way to handle these small conflicts. Conflicts of this nature are constantly coming up and robbing us of productivity. We end up spending too much time worrying about things we don't need to be worrying about and being upset about things that should not be a part of work. We need to give employees a good work environment where they can be creative and productive.

> *#7 Be aware of the carrier of hidden agendas. His fertile ground is usually around the coffee pot or water fountain and is always informal.*

No Communication Between Jobs, Departments and Divisions, or Between Management, Employees, and Unions

A lot of this has to do with fear—the number one problem in any organization. You start pitting employees against employees, management against employees, management against unions, and unions against employees. It's straight across the board and everyone is pointing fingers. It's always everyone else's fault. That is what happens when you don't have open and honest communication between everyone working with the company.

One-Way Communication

One thing that is noticeable when there is lack of communication is a lot of one-way communication. Usually informal processes funnel information through. The communication, however, becomes one-way, from the top down. It appears to be dictatorial—mandating what you're going to do. It is usually addressed informally or in memo form. There is usually no way to manage or monitor what's coming down the pipe, so your frustration builds.

Memos Not In Writing Or Well Thought Out

Most of the communication that you have in memo form is not very well written or well thought out. A lot of times you have a tendency to pass policy down through memos, but it was never intended for memos. There is no way to manage and monitor policy, because there is no system in place. Yes, a memo is a good communication device in a company, but it should not be a formal way of communicating policies and procedures. Before sending it out, you might want to get someone who doesn't have anything to do with the subject of the memo to critique it and provide input. Sometimes, what you meant is not what you said.

Hearsay

When you deal with lack of communication, especially written, you have a lot of hearsay communication in the organization. Many employees have learned to manipulate the lack of systems or process to their own benefits, often via hidden agendas and double standards. The person who passes on the hearsay usually knows enough about what should be, and the way things are—that he can predict how people will react. He pieces together information that best fits the scenario for them. When the decision-maker gets the information, it sounds right and looks good and logical. The person has won the battle by leaking information in the fashion that best serves her needs. Her behavior is totally frustrating to other employees. They can't understand why the owner would make decisions based on hearsay. The owner is being manipulated and she really doesn't know what's happening.

What-If

Much communication involves "what-ifing" the deal to death. It usually starts with a "devil's advocate" asking what if this or that happens. That can cause a lack of idea ownership, little definition, or hesitancy to put the deal into play. You can literally what-if the idea out of existence. You kill the ideas as they come on the table. Who is next with another idea? Not me, I've already been kicked around enough.

"WHAT-IFING" THE DEAL TO DEATH

Story #8

Today, there is a terrible illness infecting all companies in America. The name of this dreaded malady is "what- ifing." It is even spreading from the work place to home.

As we go into organizations and homes, we find that no matter what deal we put on the table, the carrier of the disease starts to "what-if" the deal to death. For example, we are in a conference room and someone throws out an idea. The questions start immediately. What if the union strikes; what if the market falls; what if our competition beats us to the punch; what if the bank won't finance it? The what-ifing has begun and before you know it, the idea has been beaten to death. Everyone is looking around the room trying to figure out what happened.

The person who presented it in the first place, takes it off the table and ends up wondering why he ever thought it would work. Some people say, "Let me play the devil's advocate." They then proceed to their propositions of what if this or that should happen, etc. Personally, I think the devil's advocate thing is just a cop-out.

You start to beat the enthusiasm out of an organization, because everyone begins to pick up the habit and before you know it, no one accomplishes anything. With the company not listening to new ideas, and not getting involved in new activities and not listening to its employees, the situation turns into a dangerous disease of complacency. The old status quo doesn't want to do anything because it's safe. They know they can get by doing just what's expected and no more. All forward momentum in the company is lost.

Look at all the companies that have been in business and snoozed while the times simply passed them by. How about one of our early word processor companies? They had a lock on the keyboard and data processing industry. Sales were good, so they just kept on doing what they were doing. When sales started dropping, it was already too late. What-ifing disease is a hard thing to reverse. When there are so many competitors in the marketplace, how do you get back up and compete. It takes a lot of cash, innovation, and hard work to catch up.

What-ifing in an organization is a dangerous disease. When this happens, take a look at who this what-ifing guy is. If someone is willing to put a deal on the table and take ownership, chances are that deal is going to make it. I agree; we can't go in with rose-colored glasses. But we can't knock down the guy who is bringing in new ideas and a fresh way of thinking. Remember, most all great inventions came out of a need in the marketplace that only the inventor could see. Someone's great idea could be the next Microsoft or Apple computer.

We need to examine how we can support the idea and bring it along. Remember, we all ultimately have something to put on the table. This not only has to do with new product ideas—the new idea may be related to policies and procedures. They get beaten to death, too.

Soon, the what-ifing is all encompassing. No one wants to do anything because they know it's not going to do any good. The ideas placed on the table simply fade away. We don't know what happened to it; it just didn't get finished or rescheduled.

One of the things we talk about in our team meetings has to do with ideas. If someone throws out a new idea, the rule is: discuss how we can support that idea and help that team member be successful. We know that if we criticize it, then the next time the guy won't speak up. Remember, the life of an organization is communication and the death is lack of communication.

One thing my system does is awareness-training concerning what-ifing. We teach people to think how they would feel if the idea were theirs and someone said it was stupid. Awareness goes a long way in battling this disease.

Hopefully, your company and/or department hasn't become an idea-killer or a deal-killer. There is nothing worse than an organization that is not breathing new life into their company. If everything is "business as usual," it becomes stale and unproductive.

The other bad side to this "what-ifing" problem is when you take it home with you. It's a bad habit that carries over to your wife and children and soon communication in the home dries up. The family unit shuts down, because no matter what they say, you "what-if" it to death. I cannot stress enough what a serious negative "what-ifing" can become both at work and in one's personal life. It is a habit that must be broken.

> #8 *What-ifing the deal to death is a danger, and a perilous disease for an organization.*

HOW DO WE ADDRESS THE LACK OF COMMUNICATION?

There are numerous ways to address the lack of communication in a company. I'll present several for your consideration.

Remove the Fear

You've heard enough about fear I won't beat that horse anymore.

Interpersonal Skill Training

Interpersonal skill training involves how your employees present themselves, how they receive information, and such basic things as how you look, shake hands, and display body language. Managers must acquire interpersonal skills to teach to the employees. Written communication must be positive. Instead of writing a memo that is negative, write one that is constructive and positive.

Positive Attitude

Your communication should always display a positive attitude. In doing so, the receiver usually reciprocates.

Open and Honest

Remember the BaseValues!

S.M.I.L.E.

Remember, in the INTRODUCTION, I said I would explain this later? Well, it's later.

The first half hour in the morning sets the tone for the rest of the day. So let's start out being happy and communicating. Would you believe it is contagious? ***S.M.I.L.E.*** means *"a **S**mile in the **M**orning **I**mproves **L**ife **E**veryday."*

Attack the Issues—Nothing Else

When resolving issues, attack the issues and not the employees or departments. Let's work on resolving problems not pointing the finger or pinning the blame.

Two-Way Communication or Free Flow

The best communication is that which is honest, open, and flows in two directions! This is what we call "Free Flow of information."

Twice As Much Listening As Talking

Are you familiar with the old saying about why God gave us two ears and one mouth? Yes, I know, you've heard it. God gave us two ears and one mouth so we could listen twice as much as we talk. Try practicing that Advice—do twice as much listening as you do talking. Remember to make the communication two ways. When someone is responding—listen; don't cut them off.

THE RESULTS

By using this system, you are moving from an informal to a formal organization. You will move from implied to written procedures. The work environment changes to one of employees *talking to* and *communicating with* one another. *Employees* become open, happy, and communicative *people*.

Ninety-eight percent of the problems in an organization are due to the lack of verbal and/or written communication and/or implied procedures which all fall within the four barriers to quality.

3
LACK OF WRITTEN PROCEDURE

There are 16 products/outcomes of utilizing implied procedure (verbal procedure—not in writing). They are as follows:

Informal Organization

Systems and processes, because they are not in writing, are informal. When you have implied procedures, there is a great deal of inefficiency. Things are being done two, three, and four times, and sometimes several people are doing the same thing. A great show of inefficiency is on display.

Poor Training For the Job

When you don't have written procedures, how can you have training for the BaseWork Center? You can't! Most of the training you're doing is on-the-job training, business as usual. The typical training modus operandi (M.O. for you crime buffs) is, "I'll train you with what I can remember today, and the rest you can learn on the job tomorrow."

You Can't Improve Until You Define

You can't improve until you define the way you're doing business. If the work procedure is informal or defined poorly in a BaseWork

Center, then that particular issue is continually moving. What's acceptable one day is not acceptable the next.

Bad Data

You can't improve using bad data. If none of the systems or processes has been nailed down with hard data, then their steps will be inconsistent and not properly defined. Decisions made using bad data will always be bad decisions.

Process and Systems Interpretation

Minus written procedure, perception *rules*! Three people doing the same job will have three different perspectives of that process, system, or BaseWork Center. You will have people consistently applying different interpretations to the same BaseWork Center day in and day out. Informal organizations don't work.

Bad Statistical Process Control (SPC)

When you haven't formalized your system, process, or procedures, the data collected for SPC purposes is very suspect. It will be inconsistent because you haven't formalized exactly what that system is.

No Continuous Improvement

Continuous improvement of what? How can you improve what you haven't defined? There is no continuous improvement without written procedure.

Putting Out Fires

You're continuously putting out fires. You are moving from day to day without direction. The crisis and procedure of the day is the fire of the day. Your particular fire depends on when you get up and go to the office.

Reactive Seat-of-the-Pants Running of the Business

You can't be pro-active because you can't plan or schedule. Nothing has been agreed upon in writing. There's no formal structure in the organization. Literally, you step up to the line every morning wondering what fire you're going to put out. Usually the fire creates chaos throughout the organization because, directly or indirectly, everyone is responsible or has something to do with it.

No Accountability

One day one person is responsible, the next day another is responsible. A person not being held accountable is a big frustration for employees. Employees get discouraged over the absence of accountability because it is constantly getting them in trouble.

DOUBLE STANDARDS

Story #9

Double standards exist in a corporation because there are no systems or processes in place. There is no way to monitor those systems and processes that do exist, or the existing procedures are too vague and inconsistent. Double standards destroy employee morale. I miss work and am reprimanded when I come back. It doesn't matter that I have a very valid excuse for missing, or I have taken a sick day coming to me. The double standard rears its ugly head when we have another employee that continually misses work, and his supervisor does not reprimand him, and he is not held accountable.

There are exceptions to every rule, but in a double standard situation one or two percent consistently push the issues, and are not held accountable—they miss work or a meeting and are not held accountable for it. Someone else doesn't show up for a meeting and they're reprimanded for it. That builds resentment among the employees as they talk to each other. It's usually the same person, employee, manager or department that is not being held accountable. The double standard eats at the morale of the organization. That is why I say the biggest thing a company can do to promote trust is to be consistent. If we've got a policy, we must hold everybody accountable for that policy.

Yes, certain things can come up which cannot be prevented. Certainly, we need to be flexible, but the program's position is, if it happens every other month, then there's a problem and it must be addressed.

If there are double standards such as:"I'm held accountable for my month-end statements, but the other person isn't; Our department has to meet the budget; the other departments don't; We have to hold a weekly meeting, but the other department only has it every other week;" or there is an experienced employee that misses work on Fridays or Mondays and is not held accountable, then your company has problems. These are the things that destroy the morale of an organization. It literally comes down to the fact that we have no systems and processes in place or we're not managing and monitoring the ones we do have in place.

People can be threatened by employees that are there to do a good job and work hard. There are hidden agendas for the one percent who want the good employee removed. This creates a double standard also. They work on planting negatives and lies to make the good employees look bad. This is really disheartening for an employee that does work hard, and then is being held accountable for something for which he's not responsible.

Many times double standards aren't addressed because it's easier to ignore than to take care of it. People think no one will notice. That's not true, though. Someone is processing that paperwork or Purchase Order for the entertainment tab of $105 when the standard is only $50.

We cannot have double standards. Management must lead and set the example. Management has to be in the forefront of leadership for the organization. The smallest things in a company can gnaw at the majority of employees. Up to five percent of employees create the double standard. This is created by them not being held accountable or because there is a lack of systems and processes. When the monitoring begins, the number will drop to one percent and the funnel concept process will eventually take care of them.

#9 Double standards are the quickest way to deflate a company's morale.

No Ownership of Job/BaseWork Center

There is no ownership of process, steps, procedures or systems because nothing is defined. Everything in the organization is still

45

floating around due to lack of procedure and is up to interpretation. Accountability is up for grabs.

No Monitoring

How can you monitor what hasn't been defined?   What do you monitor, if nothing has been defined and there are endless inconsistencies?

Hands-On Management

This is one of the things that happen with implied procedure. Everyone is bumping heads and stepping on top of each other. The frustration comes about when management tries to do everything themselves and they end up being hands-on managers instead of monitoring and leading. They're in the middle of it—with all the other employees putting out the fires.

No Delegating

You can't delegate anything. Why? Because when you delegate in an informal organization, then specifics are left up to interpretation by whoever is delegated. Most managers have tried that before and it doesn't work. They find it easier to just do it themselves.

Outdated Procedure

If you're not addressing the four barriers to quality and you do have procedures, then they're probably outdated or they've been written by an outside organization or the manufacturer. That usually means the use of technical language that no one in a BaseWork Center understands. After all, the employees had nothing to do with putting it together.

The Technical Procedure

A technical procedure written by engineers for a particular process just doesn't work—especially on the floor when you have employees that can't understand the terminology and it doesn't really flow with how they're actually doing the job. Remember, the technical procedures are usually written for the operation of the equipment but not for actually moving the product through the BaseWork Center or the process. You're looking at it in two different ways—how to operate equipment versus how to run manufacturing. Yes, you do need the technical information, but you also need the procedure for actual job accomplishment.

HOW DO WE ADDRESS THE LACK OF WRITTEN PROCEDURE?

Remove the Fear

You have to remove the fear. Need I say more?

Have Open and Honest Communication

You have to have open and honest communication between everyone in the company. The free flow of information is important.

Move From Implied to Written Procedure

If you move from implied to written procedures, then the best place to start is the BaseWork Centers (BW/C). You're now formalizing the way you're doing business.

Procedures Written by BaseWork Center on How to do the Job

The employees can best define how to do a job by defining their BaseWork Center. They reach agreement on the definition of the job. Even though there may be only four different people doing the same BaseWork Center, you would be amazed at the different interpretations, when they start, how they start, what they do first.

A lot of time this affects the product/service. The procedures written on the BW/C should be the consensus of the people doing the work.

System Breakdown by BaseWork Center

The systems are now broken down by BaseWork Centers. They can include everything from Purchase Order origination to processing, or from receiving raw materials through production and delivery. If you break the system down by BaseWork Center, then it becomes more manageable. Instead of the manager who's already overworked and overstressed, you now have one who has all his employees focusing on their area of expertise and control.

Processes, Steps, and Procedures

The BaseWork Centers need to be broken down by processes, steps of the processes, and the procedures of those processes, all written in the employees' terminology. The BaseWork Center is held accountable for the processes, steps and procedures. The employees also have additional duties: daily, weekly, monthly, and as needed.

Monitor the Systems

You can start monitoring the systems because you have agreed upon and documented the systems. You've formalized the way you're doing business.

Accountability

Now you've got a handle on what you are expecting to monitor. Accountability, for a change, has a face and name.

Ownership

With all the thousands of things happening in the facility, there is somebody that is now responsible and accountable and has ownership of that particular process, step, procedure, or system.

THE RESULTS

What is the end result of written procedure? You will have defined every process, step, procedure and system within the organization. Then a lot begins to happen. You get people to start thinking about their jobs and then you're defining jobs. Just by defining it, you begin to improve the process, step, procedure and systems within the organization. Now people have ownership and something in writing to start working on. You can look at improving the systems because now you have them defined in the terminology that your employees and team members understand. You've got a system that is in control.

Employee involvement is one of the greatest things that happens. When I visited companies with other quality programs, the programs started bombarding employees with difficult terminology. It had to be learned and translated to apply it to the current job. My program gets the employee to talk about himself, his job, process, and steps. When they get to talking, everyone has input. They start working towards an agreement and talking out loud. Immediately there is employee involvement in the team meetings.

Every process, step, procedure and system in the organization is now accountable and every employee will hold each other accountable for quality. In turn, because of the rules you set in place, it starts to break down the walls between divisions, departments, jobs, management, employees, and unions. Now you all have something in common to talk about. You've worked on the fear. You've worked on the communication, and now you're able to communicate without attacking.

You have a workable way of doing business now. The company is defined in the terminology that is used daily by its employees. You now have the BaseWork Center terminology in the language of the employees performing the job. That makes it easier for people to understand and comprehend.

The procedures are written by the employees that are doing the job. That creates ownership and pride within themselves because they are building a formalized organization that they have had input into and are now a part of. ***That is key. Their input is valued and trusted.***

Now that you've formalized, you can look at statistical process controls and continuously improve the way that you're doing business because everything in the organization is defined. It no longer takes massive doses of management or outside consultants to improve business. You can do it internally. Instead of one manager trying to handle 15 different BaseWork Centers, you have 15 BaseWork Centers working in coordination with the manager. That promotes leadership.

You now have total quality management. Throughout the organization, you are dealing with quality in every process, step, procedure, and system within that organization because you have also worked through the fear, the lack of communication, and now the written procedure.

4
LACK OF TRAINING

THE PRODUCT OF LACK OF TRAINING

A usual scenario finds no budget for training. Most companies that I visit not only don't know on what to train, but they don't have any idea what to budget for training. You need to set a budget and a time line for company training.

Some companies take a hit-and-miss approach to training. They see something that kind of applies and figure *that* training is better than no training at all. If you get something out of it, they guess it's okay. That kind of hit-and-miss training is very expensive.

There is no commitment from the top with training. The problem with this is that you have a CFO or CEO who sees it as an expense or a line item. It is usually the first to be cut from the budget. That is really inefficient and shows up in informal businesses.

Many companies never really get started with a training program. They all say in the beginning that they're going to have a training program because the other company they were with didn't have one. They resolve to start one, but they don't start training. The CEO is trying to make it all happen, but it just never gets started.

Training is viewed as an expense and not an asset. That is an attitude with some companies. You have to look at training as the cost of doing business. You need to determine what training you need. That's a big question with most companies. They don't know what to start with or how to get a handle on it, but they do know that they need training. Again, you're taking "off-the-shelf stuff", or whatever someone brings in that sounds good. You end up throwing indirect training at your employees. Most training products go in their own direction and are not necessarily job-specific. That means you buy one training program for an employee or a BaseWork Center or for different departments. That training terminology is not going in any particular direction. In fact, they could be going in opposite directions. There are no training tools in the organization.

How do you get started training? You can't even train on how to do your job. Most of the time the training is verbal. There's no consistency or direction in regard to the terminology of the training or the scheduling of the training. It's kind of hit and miss, month by month, quarter by quarter. You fall into the "flavor of the month" training, whatever happens to be hot or whatever has been talked about. The consultants repackage, and reword it. They sell it by saying, "If you don't have it, your whole world will fall apart."

You then have totally inefficient training dollars. You're trying your best to train and you're doing what you can with what's out there. But those dollars are probably 60% inefficient. Because there is no training, there's no cross-training. In what do you cross-train, if you don't have a training program and don't have things done.

THE COMPANY HELD
ACCOUNTABLE FOR QUALITY

Story #10

I was involved in a situation with a company hat had a lot of franchisees selling their product. One of the things that the managers of that company wanted was quality because they heard a lot about it around the industry. They wanted a quality program because everybody else had one.

This company wanted to be a quality company. The Board of Directors met and purchased an existing quality program. It sounded and looked good. It was packaged well, and it was using all the right buzz words. The people selling it to the Board were professional salesmen. They were convinced it was the product for them. The recommendation went down through the company to buy and implement the program.

It was just like many of the existing programs. The company management wrote grand mission statements, goals, and ways that they wanted to conduct business. They looked good and sounded good and managers were so proud of them. The statements were tacked up for everyone to see.

The sad thing was that almost every employee walked through those doors, looked at the statements, and just shook their heads. They didn't believe it was going to happen.

Even though the intent was good, it would never filter down through the organization. They weren't good programs. They tell you a lot of different information, but they don't tell you how to get there.

As the company moved through their quality program, it filtered down. They got direct or indirect feedback that the program was working. They reported back to the president of the company that they had quality. The president reported to the CEO the same thing. The CEO sent back to the Board that his company had quality and everyone felt good, patting themselves on the back. They never went down on the floor to see if they really did have quality.

The upper management of this company talked themselves in circles until they believed they didn't have any problems or the problems were someone else's. What this company did was convince themselves they had quality, but their franchisees and dealers didn't have quality. They were blamed for making a mess of things.

The franchisees, dealers, and associate companies then began to hold the primary company accountable for quality. What the company said and what they actually did were two different things, and that was non-quality. Based on what the company had in writing—who they were and what they were doing—the dealers expected quality. Their dealers and franchisees were now holding them accountable.

The primary company started justifying and defending themselves and a wall went up between the company and their dealers and franchisees. It became apparent they were saying one thing but doing another. Everyone was blaming everyone else for the issues and problems and before you knew it, the quality program no longer existed.

The perception was that it just didn't work for them and didn't pertain to their business. They rationalized that their dealers and franchisees were quality and the issue just faded away. Faded away, that is, until they found another quality program that told them what they wanted to hear. They just couldn't stand up and be held accountable.

This is what happens in companies when they take on a program internally. They want to implement quality. The employees start holding them accountable for quality and before you know it, the whole thing blows up. They let it pass and move on to another "flavor of the month."

Accountability is sometimes hard to take. My hat is off to the companies with which I've contracted that have a strong entrepreneur/CEO. He/she has made the decision to be held accountable. The reason they did so is because they were wonderful people who really cared and had no hidden agendas. They wanted to do the right thing.

It is simple, but then it isn't. If you look at it—who doesn't want to do the right thing? We are talking about 99% that do. How do you make it happen internally in an organization? It's tough to make it happen and we usually don't give it enough time or direction.

When we start holding one another accountable, then it gets uncomfortable and we pin the blame on everyone else. Soon, we aren't carrying through the program. Our employees are left holding the bag again with another inconsistent program. They expended a lot of effort and energy in the program and it got them nowhere. As they began trying to hold everyone accountable, they thought they were now singled out as being a problem-maker. That is sad.

#10 What is good for the goose is sometimes hard to swallow for the gander.

DON'T BUY BEFORE YOU IDENTIFY

Story #11

When we are buying equipment, software, or computer products, we need to define what we need and what standards of quality we expect. I'll use, as an example, something we need to practice throughout the organization.

Assume we are buying a software program. What happens in many software companies after you buy their package? They come in and go through a very comprehensive training program. They gather all the employees together and go over everything the program does. It sounds good, you say you understand everything, and the trainer walks out the door. In reality, few people grasped what the guy was talking about. What do we do now?

At this point, most companies resort to using the technical manual as a training tool. Most employees, when they learn the computer, want to learn only the functions for which they are responsible. The trainer, however, did not instruct personnel in that fashion.

The company needs to ensure that the salesman breaks down and explains the software according to BaseWork Centers. Teach the people in accounts receivable accounting, the people in the warehouse inventory control, etc. If you do that and focus on it, then you can cross-train one another once everyone has mastered his/her particular function.

Try to get someone in customer service at the computer company to help with a problem. I guarantee you they will just point to the manual. Buying a system and relating it to how you are doing business are two different things. Get the salesman to break it down before the purchase—he isn't likely to do it afterwards. He is out selling and turning more deals. If you buy a piece of equipment, then the same thing holds. It has operating procedures. Let's break it down by jobs and understand it before purchasing it. Make sure that part of the sales agreement is breaking it down and understanding it according to the BaseWork Center.

Before making the purchase look at the equipment in terms of the BaseWork Center. You need to tell the company what your needs are and insist that they match their product to the workplace. It's too late to negotiate after it's been purchased. Everyone gets frustrated and oftentimes the equipment is not used efficiently.

> #11 *Do not buy any product or service that does not define its training by the company's BaseWork Centers or jobs.*

HOW DO WE ADDRESS LACK OF TRAINING?

You have to remove the fear and have open and honest communication. You have to move to written procedures, and you must get a commitment from top management, in regard to the training program. They must sign-off that training is important. You have to budget at least 2% to 6% of payroll to training. That's a good number with which to begin.

BUDGET TWO TO SIX PERCENT

Story #12

The business place is an interesting world, especially when it comes to training budgets. Would you believe that most companies haven't a clue as to the content of critical training, little ability to successfully start their training program, or how much to budget? I'm obviously talking a training plan here.

Based on the research I have done and verified by my clients, a company should budget between two and six percent of payroll for training. They also need to budget two to four hours of training per month per employee, for at least the first 24 months of the program.

Long-term planning will instill required discipline into most companies' training plan process. Typically, companies have not planned more than a week or two, or maybe a month in advance. Using this approach, the planning process includes not only budgeting funds, but also budgeting time.

When preparing a budget for training, many have a tendency to look at the man-hours that will be spent in training, especially if we have accountants looking at the figures. Their comment is often, "Look what it is costing us having that employee out of work." Or they may worry that it shuts down production. The latter problem is fairly easy to solve. Production simply tells us the best time for them to schedule the training meetings. Everyone involved in scheduling the meetings makes their own decisions.

We will also address the "what if's?" What if a customer comes in? We will address each of these issues one at a time. We know that 40% of the work day is wasted. If you want to step back and look at it, I tell CEO's that they will become two to four hours a month more efficient. The reason: people become more efficient once they start planning, scheduling and holding these meetings. When we start looking at formalizing our training program, it is alarming to look at the loss of man-hours. This is especially true when everyone complains about being so busy and overworked. Keep in mind the labor statistics, though. Forty percent of the work day is wasted because of inefficiency.

What we see is that we must plan better, have better scheduling and hold everybody accountable. Don't defeat the training program based on soft budgeted dollars. If we can get management to sit and budget our training, then usually it is deemed a dollar well spent.

Again, we have to get started. A company must be committed to training. Yes, it is going to cost money, but that is the cost of doing business. There is never a good time to start, or a time when it's comfortably affordable. It will work, if you bite it off a little at a time and keep your program moving in the right direction. The key is to get started!

> #12 *Do not look at the training budget as an expense, but as an investment and an asset of your company.*

You can educate your trainers from within. You don't really need to go on the outside to get people to train your employees once you start defining your BaseWork Centers.

You need to set the schedule for your training a year in advance. That is one of the first formal things with which the company will struggle.

Most managers don't schedule much in their day-to-day operation. The scheduling will be good discipline. It will force managers to schedule at least the one or two days a month for the next year. They will have to think through this with their employees. Once you get into training, most managers will discover that they don't even know where their employees are, what they're doing, or what schedule they're on in a given day. It takes a tremendous amount of effort to know who's doing what and where. Trying to put it together usually takes a team effort because employees will have to plan around production. They will have to make those decisions.

You have to train the personnel in regard to interpersonal skills and communication, planning and management, self-help, as well as process, steps, procedures, and systems training.

There has to be someone in charge of the training. You could call them the Coordinator. Somebody has to be responsible. It doesn't necessarily have to be the human resource person, but someone must be in charge.

Once training is in process, you begin to have employees cross-training one another. They're trained on their particular job, they've defined their jobs around their BaseWork Centers, now they can cross-train one another starting with the internal customer and supplier— the people from whom you're receiving and to whom you're giving your work. This is a great tool. Now you can manage and monitor training and cross-training.

EXISTING TRAINING

Story #13

I have found that when going into companies, the smaller ones don't know what training they need. They do know they need training but aren't necessarily sure where to start. They also have no idea how to budget for training. If you don't budget and schedule the training, it's just not going to happen.

What I have found is that companies need to set aside two to six percent of payroll costs for training. By doing that, they now have a budget. The budget allows them to realistically look at what they can afford, based on their needs for training.

The problem with most of management, however, is that they have no tool to direct this training. How do they decide what to do? The training that exists in the marketplace goes in all kinds of directions. If they're not careful, they end up with a training program that covers a lot of areas but doesn't really go in any particular direction.

Training without direction can cause a company to continually stop and start training without really knowing where they're going with it. They also don't know with what they'll end up.

Companies don't consider training expense because they haven't budgeted for it. Many of our owners realize they have things wrong in their company, but they are so busy holding it together, they can't deal with it. Since they can't afford a human resource person, everything, including training, gets put on the back burner. Usually, it's too late before they figure out how they are going to change things. Only training and education can change this situation.

I can help the company develop a basis for a training program for the entire organization. When we start, we know exactly what we're going to do. We have a step-by-step process that we manage and monitor. Since the process is carefully documented, then we know what the end result will be.

We will end up with every system, process, procedure, job, structure, and employee documented and trained within a 24-month period. We know that in order to improve business, we first have to define it. A training program must be focused, directed, managed, and monitored. It must start with the end in mind. My system has on-site research and development to create the Base Training Program for the entire organization.

> #13 *The best people to help you design what is needed for training internally within your organization are your employees and that person doing the particular task.*

THE RESULTS

You have pro-active training—you know where you're going to start; you know what it's going to cost; you know who's going to be involved; and you know when they're meeting. Instead of reacting to problems, you're now going through the organization with pro-active training. You formalize the employee training through the written procedures. Now you have something for training new hires because you have BaseWork Centers, processes, steps, and procedures. You can formalize the cross-training and manage and monitor the new hire training and cross-training. How many times have you seen someone get a little bit of training and then they're thrown out into the workplace? They're going to get the rest on the job, or you say you'll do the rest next week, but you never do because you're too busy putting out fires.

You'll have new leadership appear as a result of training from within. You will have people step up internally in your organization and take the program and run with it. You will now be budgeted in one direction with a committed training program. You all know where you're going, when you're going to be meeting, and on what you're working. It is in user-friendly terms. Everyone can talk about it. Everyone knows what the training is and it becomes a part of your daily life—day in and day out.

Training can be continuously improved, delegated, and monitored because now you have systems, processes, and scheduling throughout the organization. In fact, you can have one employee in a job that is cross-training or a new hire responsible for that training because he knows how to do his job. Now he can perform it or train someone for it because it's in writing. You can now build a whole company of trainers.

You now have the tools for effective training. Your training within the organization is now job-specific, budgeted, and on a schedule. Everyone is getting interpersonal skills training. Management is scheduled for training. There is process, step, procedure, system and BaseWork Center training. Your entire company can go from one training class to another because the terminology and direction is the same. If a guy misses one class, he can catch up at another class because every class will be on a particular process and step. The guy can plug in his particular job to that training class. You can't shut down production in order to do training. But that will, in fact, help you manage and schedule your production along with whatever else is happening internally within that organization.

You come out of this with a formalized training program for new hires, for cross-training, for monitoring. It's a continual, on-going process. As the employees learn more, they come up with more ideas, and believe me, you are now looking at a company where everyone is more aware, and is doing business in a formalized business structure and environment. All the four barriers are enforced, supported, reinforced, and talked about daily.

THE SIX SUPPORTS OF QUALITY

A Positive Note

Written Procedure with input from the employees that are doing the job gives the workers the ability to use their knowledge effectively and readily, in the execution or performance of that job. You now have craftsmen taking pride in their work and accomplishments.

Bruce

WHAT'S NEXT?

By now, I'm sure you can see the validity of the four barriers to quality. You're probably saying to yourself, however, "Even if I buy into your theory, how do I resolve my company's quality issues? Where do we start the journey toward quality?"

In your quest for quality, you must understand the importance of "Change."

5
ORGANIZATIONAL CHANGE

DEFINITION OF CHANGE

What exactly is change? **Change** is *to become different or alter, transform or convert the way that you're currently doing business.* In my system, change usually means moving from an informal to a formal organization by building the business infrastructure.

Change must have unquestionable commitment, desire, and leadership from the top tier of company management. Just try going into a department and suggesting change. Because of the existing way a company has been doing business, there is a tremendous amount of fear. One issue of concern to employees is fear of the need to define their job. A common misconception is that after they define the job in great detail, the company will find someone for less money to take over. Management is also afraid! Their misconception is that, if every employee does their job and is responsible for their own jobs, then why do you need managers? Is there any other fear? You 'betcha' there is! The union is thinking, "if everyone is getting along, why do you need the union?" Fear, whether rational or not, is very common when you go into companies and propose change. There are, however, people who will face their fear and step up to get things going internally within the organization.

CHANGE IS FEAR

Story #14

Any change in an organization brings fear. The reason most people react with fear is because there is uncertainty relating to the outcome. For the most part, experience has told employees that with change comes some sort of hidden agenda, or possibly even the down-sizing of the company. This makes them resistant to change.

It's usually easier, and seems safer, just to continue manufacturing the product and do what we have always done—rather than to change. We know a sure thing, but change is risky business! As we discussed earlier, one of the only ways companies know how to promote change is to cut expenses, and that causes fear.

My program is 74 hours of classes conducted over a 24-month period. I feel that change is both mental and emotional. It's not just changing the way we do business, our jobs, or the processes. We, as individuals, have to change and learn to deal with that change. We need certain skills and/or tools to help cope with the change. This is why I offer workshops on interpersonal and communication skills. Employees may look at things and say the work environment is bad, but it is easier for them to keep on, than it is to change. This is true because our current comfort-zone centers on coping with the bad work environment. Anything else is likely to cause uncertainty and fear.

The biggest things we need to do when we go into an organization is have that change well thought out, communicated, planned, directed, monitored, and have the employees involved. Most change in corporate America is derived without input from employees. It comes from management demanding the employees do certain things, and the employee shake their heads because it makes no sense, and there seems to be no justification. They're not involved, and they feel it is being crammed down their throats.

If a company gets their employees involved along the way, there will be less resistance to change, and employees will improve greatly. They will hold one another accountable for quality, they will write tougher procedures, they will work harder on the processes and systems, and they will perform better than management could ever hope for.

There is no room for micro-management in a good quality program. A few individuals cannot make it all happen. All employees must be involved. We can hammer the employees all day long, but until they see consistency and get used to the change, there will be resistance. Never forget—**change causes fear!**

The best way to bring about change is constant reinforcement—explaining where the process leads, documenting the plans of that change, and doing what we say we're going to do. Consistency promotes trust, and helping the employees accept this change emotionally eliminates fear.

#14 *The only way change is going to happen in an organization is for an employee to feel secure in that organization.*

Change is a slow process that needs constant reinforcement in the organization. The only way it is going to happen is through proper communication and understanding. Change is fear. You have to constantly reinforce your employees concerning where the company is going and how it's going to get there.

THE PROFILE OF CHANGE

There is a profile to change. For change to occur, numerous things have to be in place.

Leadership

The first ingredient in the profile of change is **Leadership.** Top management must be actively leading and directing the transition from an informal to a formal organization, focusing on the four barriers to quality. It must come from the top—the CEO, the Board of Directors, and the owner of the organization. No one is going to move without the boss signing off on the deal. Once you have your bosses sign a letter explaining what will happen, their support will be very evident.

The business of business is constantly changing; there is a lot happening in the marketplace. One of the things happening is called redesigning or re-engineering. That is not what my program is about. Re-engineering isn't the tool that management needs in the transformation of change; they need something else.

I feel company leadership has to have a new tool. One that builds jobs instead of destroying them. BaseWork Systems 2000 is the answer to their dilemma. Unlike re-engineering, it answers questions such like: When do we start? What will happen? How do we manage and monitor? What is the expense and with what will we end up? By giving leadership an effective tool, change can happen.

Concession

Concession is the second tool. The company and its leadership have to yield to or grant change. Leadership must accept the need for it. The employees won't accept it until management does; how can they? It has to come from leadership. Employees have to have the concession that they are going to change and understand what it is that will be changing. They should be told of the change from an informal to a formal organization where the focus will be on eliminating the four barriers to quality.

Commitment

Next is **commitment.** The company's leadership needs to makes a promise to follow the two fundamental rules of BaseValues concepts: 1) do what is morally and ethically correct and 2) treat everybody as you want to be treated. Change needs total commitment. The biggest problem with commitment is employee experience. Many companies haven't been very good in the past about honoring commitment. It gets put on the table and then soon the commitment is no longer there. It is forgotten and they move on to the next sense of urgency.

Again, commitment from the organizational perspective has to come from and begin with top management. It has to be communicated downward in writing to all the managers. They have to support and help promote the profile of change. Employees will follow from day one but they will be hesitant and reserved because they're waiting to see the commitment demonstrated. Commitment holds everybody accountable. No one can be exempt from pursuing quality or from change. Once the commitment of the leadership of the company is evident, you'll get the commitment from everybody else.

AFFIRMATION

Story #15

Affirmation is, for example, when we say we're not going to spit in public. We've said it, now how do we actually accomplish the goal? We start by reminding and repeating to ourselves several times a day not to spit in public. It will probably take eight or nine months before the non-spitting behavior becomes part of our subconscious. After that, we're doing it automatically and we don't have to repeat it. Affirmation has become a habit. There is probably some other clinical term for it, but that's what happens.

If it takes eight or nine months to reinforce something as simple as not spitting in public, how can we change an organization's habits in six months or even one year? If you are doing something for six to eight months in a company, then you are showing signs of consistency. In eight months to a year you are moving in the right directions, but there is still a great deal that you're trying to put together.

With my program, in 12 to 18 months, we see a lot of change because that's when the Base Work Centers are taking shape and have been defined and finalized. The problems begin to vanish and fear is almost history. The written procedures are on target and the training is continuing and consistent. So, within 18 to 24 months you have a program that's going to stay and you've got a commitment that it will stay.

Actually, the company has little choice in whether or not the program stays after that time period. Why? Because once the people have made the transition, they will not allow it to turn back.

A good analogy is Communism. There has been concern about people going back to Communism because of how bad things are in some of the countries. It'll never happen! Why you ask? Because once the people have had a taste of freedom, they won't go back. There is too much awareness now via satellite and more information getting out to these people every day. They are too well informed to want to go back.

Let's get back to affirmation. Once the company turns the corner on quality and removes the four barriers, it will be very difficult to reverse. The secret to the change working is consistency. The change has to be consistent, well thought out, and it has to be gradual.

If someone is talking to you and saying that they can change your corporate culture in one seminar or by sending your managers somewhere, that's just not possible. You can't learn it in class. You must take it back to the workplace and constantly reinforce it day in and day out. That's what quality awareness is.

We've got to talk about the four barriers to quality and the way we're doing the job. There must be training and skill development. A seminar won't cut the mustard! We have to keep it constantly in front of us either in writing, during class, or whatever. If not, we soon forget, and another program goes by the wayside.

#15 *The path of change is taken a step at a time and measured in miles and months.*

Consistency

Consistency should be next in line. Consistency usually starts showing after there is a commitment. Now for the first time, the organization is consistent day in and day out with everything it takes on. Most new procedures and programs in an organization fall by the wayside within three to six months. Consistency is extremely important. It will become evident once you start seeing leadership in the organization.

The employees are hungry to see everybody united and doing the right thing. With consistency, everyone has to be accountable to the same principles and practices. You have to have a consistent behavior from leadership—then all the employees will jump on board. How do you get consistency? You get it by showing commitment and concessions that are driven by leadership.

Truth

Truth is the fifth ingredient. Management must be truthful with employees. Truth suggests conformity between statement of facts and reality. You see truth when you see consistency. If you are consistent, you are being truthful with your employees. As you move through change, it is very important that you are truthful, explaining what's happening during the transition.

The employees must feel you are being truthful and honest with them. If so, then they buy in. You have to walk the walk and talk the talk. You can no longer say one thing and do another. If you say you're going to do what is morally and ethically correct and treat everybody as you want to be treated, then you have to live up to that. You cannot say it and not live it. You have to subscribe to and be a part of the change. In being truthful, you are demonstrating the honesty and integrity of the organization. The employees must feel during the transition that everything you're saying is truthful. The truth must be that you have made the concession to change and that it has the total support of the leadership.

Trust

Trust is next on the list. The employees in an organization must have a firm belief and confidence in management's honesty, integrity, reliability, and sense of justice. Faith should exist that what you're saying and doing is true. That promotes trust. Truthfulness and consistency lead to trust. When you have employees that trust you, then you can lead them anywhere because they are eager to follow. Not only

will they follow, but they will step up to leadership positions within the organization. It is important to promote trust in an organization. The simplest way to do that is to do what is right—to do what is morally and ethically correct, and to treat everybody as you want to be treated. That's the bottom line! When you have the trust of your employees—they will follow.

Motivating

Motivating your employees is key. The more trust, respect, integrity and honesty the company has, the easier it is to motivate your employees. You will move from having to motivate the employees to their automatically being motivated. They will pick up the momentum of change by starting to step out and take the leadership role. With trust, truth, consistency, commitment, concession, and leadership all in place, the employees now become self-motivated. They are excited and happy to go to work; they are now talking about work in a positive way, looking forward to doing new things, to the changes happening, and to being involved in the work place.

Motivation has to come from the leadership of the organization. It's hard to get an organization cranked up. Move your employees from the point where they *need motivating* to the point where they are *being motivated*.

Monitor

You have to **monitor** from all levels of the organization. It is necessary to keep checking and regulating what is happening within the company's transition of change.

Monitoring is a particular strength of BaseWork Systems 2000 because there is a step-by-step process that you can use to lead, manage, monitor, and hold accountable every BaseWork Center, every process, step, procedure, system, department, and division in the organization.

As you build the business infrastructure and formalize, you are not **managing** from the top, rather, you are **leading** from the top. Everyone is motivated; they trust the company. They have seen the consistency and now they will not only hold themselves accountable, but they will hold everyone else accountable. Management changes from managing to leading. You can monitor and hold accountable the entire process. If something's not happening, you deal with data.

In dealing with data, you have to figure out what's wrong and how to move it along. Everything has to be monitored by either the individual or the organization. You can't just put things into play and let them go. The easiest way to monitor is by training employees regarding what's happening.

Maintenance

Number nine is **maintenance**. Once you have the change process up and running, then you have to continue with it. Not only is it a big job to get it up and going, but it is also difficult to maintain the forward momentum.

You now have a formal organization and you've attacked the four barriers. Now you have to maintain where you are, what you're doing, the current way you're doing business, and the program. The easiest way to do that is for everyone in the organization to concentrate on maintaining their BaseWork Center and their process, steps, and procedures. That concept is sometimes difficult for top management because they are building-oriented, not maintenance-oriented. By building the strength in the organization the leader/CEO can now keep building. Now she has an organization, that can maintain and monitor *and* is self-motivated. She can do her BaseWork Center, which is to build the organization.

Accountability

Accountability is a key tool. You are now obliged to account for your actions, your BaseWork Center, and your process, steps, and procedures. Because you are moving from an informal to a formal organization, you are now capable of being accountable. Everything is explainable. Now you are **able** to be responsible.

One of the biggest things I hear in companies is that employees don't want to be held accountable. As you go into different departments you'll hear employees say, "It's not my job; it's not my responsibility." The reason for that is sometimes they are held accountable and given the responsibility and sometimes they aren't. They may get into trouble for their process and system. They are held accountable for things over which they have no control or responsibility.

Your organization must step up to the accountability table. You have the management support to be responsible— the CEO has enabled you. The leadership starts spreading out to where everyone is holding themselves and others accountable including internal customers and suppliers. Everyone in the organization has to be held accountable for quality. Absolutely no one is exempt from doing quality. Accountability is key; there are no short-cuts or fast tracks. In this profile of change, you have to do things over weeks, months, and years to make it happen successfully.

Improvement

Next on the short list is improvement. You are improving to a better quality and condition, a better state of doing business. You must continuously improve the way you're doing business. You hear the term *continuous improvement*. You can't get that until you have the profile of change completed. Instead of continuous improvement being managed, it's being led through the organization by every employee in that organization. It now becomes something you can control. It is broken down from a complex system. You are in a position now of continuously improving business.

You do this by breaking the organization down by BaseWork Centers, processes, steps, procedures, and additional duties. You can now hold each other accountable and the program is maintaining itself. You now have the vehicles and a formalized system to monitor. You are self-motivated and trustful, not only of the company, but each other. Employees are speaking in truth with one another. You are consistent, thereby promoting commitment. How about that as a profile of change?

Awareness

Finally, you have **awareness.** Awareness is the realization and the perception of knowledge. You have a real knowledge and understanding of what's happening in the organization. Awareness is key in the organization. You've done all this, and now the employees are turned on and tuned in to where you're going, and how you're going to get there. They now possess the skills and confidence that the profiles of change have given them.

It's not the whole organization reacting to a big problem; it is now all the BaseWork Centers, processes, and systems interacting daily to deal with particular situations and issues in the organization. They are able to respond to external customers and suppliers. With awareness, you are able to respond rather than react. You are now pro-active and making things happen, and able to foresee where potential problems might occur. Each muscle in the organization is handling its own issues daily, even hourly, throughout the organization.

YOU GET OUT OF LIFE WHAT
YOU PUT INTO IT

Story #16

Growing up in Alabama, I heard repeatedly from my parents and grandparents that "you get out of life what you put into life" or "what goes around comes around." As they explained it, it seemed to make sense, but as a child I couldn't see far enough ahead to determine if it really worked. I did believe, as a child, that what my parents and grandparents said was true. Therefore, I believed that was how we should conduct ourselves.

Now, looking back through the years, there were many situations, both business and personal, where the short-term didn't make much sense. Internally, however, I was driven to follow the rule. Long-term always seemed to work out. By holding to my integrity and doing what was morally and ethically correct, and treating everybody the way I wanted to be treated, things always worked out in the long term.

What we need to do is take this same philosophy into business. We have talked throughout the four barriers to quality about all the short-term solutions, quick fixes, quotas, and new management philosophy that look good but in the long run didn't work out. Oftentimes, it was at the expense of our employees, our families, our communities, and even our country. This principle applies just as much to our business life as it does in our personal lives. Our businesses need to practice doing what is morally and ethically correct and treating everybody as you want to be treated.

> #16 *Short-term winners at the expense of another usually end up long-term losers.*

SUMMARY

As all of this is happening, you are attacking the four barriers to quality. If you are doing all of this, the four barriers to quality become a no-brainer. You now have an aware organization and you're continuously improving the way you're doing business.

PROFILE OF CHANGE

Breaking Through The 4 Barriers To Quality	Existing Way of Doing Business
Formal	**Informal**
1. Leadership	Management
2. Concession	Stand Fast
3. Commitment	Won't Take a Stand
4. Consistency	Chaos
5. Truthful	Half Truths
6. Trustful	Suspicious
7. Motivating	Demoralizing
8. Monitoring	Fire Fighting
9. Maintenance	Reaction
10. Accountability	Moving Target
11. Improvement	Status Quo

PART II

Change is really important, isn't it? You know your company must embrace it, but is that enough to ensure quality? No, it's not. It's just the beginning of a process that will probably take your company a couple of years.

Next, you must examine your current method of doing business. That's how you really get started!

In Part I, we covered the four barriers to quality. Now that the four barriers have been identified, we are in the position to begin the process of removing the barriers and moving from an informal to a formal organization.

Part II, covering chapters six through 10, focuses on describing BaseWork Systems 2000. It begins by defining corporate structure and moves the reader through corporate infrastructuring through the BaseWork Systems 2000 program. Part II also discusses BaseSkills training, both personal and professional. All employees receive BaseSkills training through One-Hour-One-Page workshops specifically designed to meet the needs of the company's employees.

Chapter 8 addresses the foundation of our program: BaseWork Centers. It is through BaseWork Centers that problems are solved, jobs are defined and redefined, and procedures are written. Chapter 10 identifies our Four Problem-Solving Processes that are unique to our BaseWork Systems 2000 program.

6
GETTING STARTED

"Building Business Infrastructures"

One of the strengths of BaseWork Systems 2000 is the ease with which you can get started—that is something makes us stand out from the crowd. Remember, we're not just talking about **what** a company should do; we're also explaining **how** they can do it. We teach the "how to" in moving a company from an informal to a formal organization via the improvement of the processes, steps, and procedures. By so doing, we direct them toward a continuous mode of improving quality in the organization.

The first thing that must be done is get the commitment of the CEO in the organization. The managers and employees will not commit without the approval of the "Big Cheese."

The company should take an in-depth look at how they're currently doing business. First, take a look (with the CEO) at your organizational chart, your chain of command, and your organizational structure. What you will see is that how things exist on the floor and how they're written down are two completely different things.

More than likely, the organization has changed (If it hadn't, that would be a new experience for me). The reason you review the existing structure is to foster understanding of the changes. When you get into problem-solving and defining BaseWork Centers, there is confusion about who's doing what. Consequently, we are now moving from consultant to resultant. Therefore, it's very important to agree on the existing structure of the organization.

CORPORATE STRUCTURE

Story #17

During my infancy as a quality resultant, I tried to model my system after the accepted school of thought in the area. In other words, I started everything off with a brainstorming session to identify problems. Boy, were we in for a surprise! One of the things that surfaced, as we were trying to determine accountability for processes and systems, was the fact that we didn't know who was responsible for the processes, either formally or informally.

That tad bit of revelation caused us to go back and define the way we were doing business—in other words, review the corporate organizational chart. The way the corporate structure existed, and the way it was perceived by employees apparently was two different things.

The CEO sitting at the top will tell you they have a formal structure and the departments will agree. When you get down to who is accountable, however, people have moved and job titles have changed. You will hear during the meetings, one person say that another is handling something but has left for another department— leaving that area unsupervised.

We tried another approach. We asked managers to plug people into where they thought they should be—because many times we didn't know what the job was. We began to build the BaseWork Center by asking identified people what they did. Finally, we had started formalizing the way we were doing business. Defining the corporate structure up front, defining the way we did business, helped us, in turn, to lay the foundation for the BaseWork Centers and the requisite accountability.

Companies say they will define the corporate structure when they get around to it, but somehow they never get around to it. When you have to start at that point, there will be frustration because everyone believes that the corporate structure already exists—that it is on the computer represented by the organizational chart. You will see that it is out-dated or just not accurate anymore. It will be, however, a good starting point.

> #17 *You cannot define jobs and BaseWork Centers, systems, or processes until you come to an agreement on the actual corporate structure. Research typically reveals that corporate structure differs from perception to reality.*

INFORMAL TO FORMAL ORGANIZATION

A lot of work must be done up-front. You've got to get the employees involved. Don't be surprised if it's hard to place people on an organizational chart. What you need to do is start organizing in relation to company needs, not personalities. People have changed jobs, departments have changed, and believe me, your organizational chart is more than likely outdated.

You need to come to an agreement on the structure. Don't get frustrated—the difference between what you think is the situation and what actually exists really starts to show up now. By starting to plug people into departments, you will set the tone for the required structure. Next, you'll start setting up BaseWork Centers and plugging employees into their jobs.

You have to get upper and middle department management involved in reviewing and coming to an agreement on the existing structure. Without this agreement everything else becomes more complex and disorganized down the road.

CORPORATE IMAGE

One of the things you must do is change corporate's image. In many instances, corporate has developed an image viewed as dictatorial. If that is the case in your company, the image must be flipped from dictatorial to participatory and supporting. The questions corporate must be willing to ask are: "In order for you to do a better job, what are the things with which we can help you? How can we support you to meet your goals and budget? What are the things corporate needs to do?" Typically, a corporate image evolves. Over time you have allowed upper and/or middle management to become very directive in their style. You were sitting and pointing fingers instead of asking how or why. You should have been asking, "How do you feel? What is the best way to do it? How can I help you to do your job better?"

Remember, the only way most employees view corporate, and the only interaction they have with corporate, is when there is a problem. When management walks into a room, there is usually a problem. Based on the historical perspective of most employees, every time management or corporate shows up, there is a problem & they are in trouble for something. Again, that is the only way the typical employee sees corporate management.

Can you understand why it's so very important that you change the corporate style from dictatorial to participatory and supportive?

TAKING OFF THE GLOVES

Story #18

The best example of "taking off the gloves" is when we were asking management to do the "S.M.I.L.E." (*a **S**mile in the Morning **I**mproves **L**ife **E**veryday*) You can imagine the reception I got. I had one manager, who was totally frustrated, come right out and say it was as much the employees' responsibility as it was his to say good morning. Everyone was pointing fingers. Our position is that nothing will happen without the support and leadership of management. Whether we like it or not, leadership has to set the tone for S.M.I.L.E., and they must be the ones to lead and guide their fellow employees.

So, we ask everyone to simply take off the boxing gloves. Leadership is here to lead the organization. Let's take the gloves off and stop jockeying for position and address the issues—not as individuals and personalities or departments—but address the issues that need resolution. Everyone must come to the table, take off the gloves and treat each other with respect. Remember, we do what is morally and ethically correct, and treat everyone as we want to be treated. Management must stand up and take the lead.

> #18 *The gloves of quality and change are worn by the hands of integrity and trust.*

RON

Story #19

I have gone into several organizations where one person wears several different hats. For example, he might be over manufacturing and have on an operations hat. He might also be in charge of sales or a particular department. Or he might be in charge of a particular location or profit-center. He is wearing many different hats—maybe too many.

I recall one situation, with a guy named Ron, who was a good performer within the organization. People start funneling more jobs to him, and because of his nature he just kept taking them. Before you know it, he had an unmanageable workload. While trying to be all things to all people, Ron became very inefficient in everything. For example, you might ask him to supply you with certain data pertaining to one segment of his job. He couldn't do it. He's too busy trying to get another loose end tied up. There is always a reason why something couldn't get done. This person is literally spinning his wheels.

Less than two percent of the population has the skill necessary to juggle that many different tasks at one time. It all started with good intentions to help out, but it became very inefficient. Now it is harmful to the company because things have started to drop through the cracks. This person may even resent someone looking at what he is doing. When you try to get him through a series of meetings or define what he does, not only is it confusing, but he may even fight and resist. He is unaccustomed to the accountability and is becoming frustrated. For the first time, he sees it taking more capacity than what he has to do all the jobs he does—and do them well.

Sometimes, the person may have worked themselves into the job with a hidden agenda. No one can put a finger on what he really does because he has built himself a nice little kingdom. This aggravates everybody around him, and people that work with him or under him get very frustrated. In defining what his job is, sometimes he will resist. As you work through the program, everyone has to come to an agreement on defining the job.

This person can hold the company hostage. He knows just enough about everything, and everyone knows too little about what he does to confront his power.

> #19 *Beware of the manager who says, "I am just so busy I can't afford to plan or schedule my day; I don't have time."*

SUMMARY

In summary, to get your company started toward quality, you have to review the existing structure and start moving the mentality of management more toward a supportive posture. The biggest thing you will see is the consistency of attitude starting to radiate, not only in the existing model, but in other divisions.

I do need to add, as a closing note, that there are many companies that are too large to have a quality program implemented corporate wide from day one. If that is the case with your company, pick a representative division or site for initial implementation. Use it to develop a model that can then be exported to the other divisions/sites.

CORPORATE MODEL

Story #20

A good quality program faces its first major decision when it encounters the organization with multiple sites. There is a problem going in and trying to implement a quality training program company-wide. Specifically, you haven't figured out how the program will interact with the organization. Many programs simply ignore the problem. They have a tendency to try and install the program without a model. On the other hand, a system like ours would never attempt such an effort without first developing the model.

Most companies want instant gratification. They want it overnight. It's just not possible when you are dealing with multiple facilities and/or multiple states. If we succumb to temptation, we roll it out too fast. The training programs aren't thought through because half the people using them aren't involved in development. The program has never been tested to determine problems and/or how to address them.

Let's say we have 10 different locations, each with 10 employees. We all of a sudden encounter a problem. Our usual way of doing business is to devise a company-wide training program to address the issue. Trying to go back and manage/monitor what is happening with one particular location is utter chaos. We spend 99% of the time readdressing and correcting the training program, and then we lose sight of what we set out to do. That adds up to inconsistency.

When we talk about building a model, let's build it around how we do business. Usually the best place to start is the corporate office. Typically, they reflect how we most commonly do business. Corporate usually has manufacturing or something on site that represents the business. If not, pick the division that best models how the company is doing business. Then develop that model.

If you have 10 different locations simultaneously trying to figure out how we do business, then it will be a fight and a struggle from day one. You will never come to an agreement. Go to one site and develop the model.

It may take a year to develop the corporate model, but once we roll it out, it can take less time to replicate at the other sites. Now we are able to manage and monitor the growth of this program internally within the organization.

Now, when we sit down at the different divisions, we have something we can manage and monitor. We now have an excellent tool as a model for training. Remember, change is fear. No matter how big or small, change creates fear and uncertainty because of the four barriers to quality. So, simply step back, develop the corporate model for doing business, get it approved, and proceed.

Corporate must support the model. It will probably change the way they are doing business. For the first time, they will have a vehicle for receiving and acting upon input. The corporate model will set the tone for change and will bring about change in an orderly manner. Every company wants to stay in business and continue to make money. That goal is best achieved through planned activity and change. Employees can only absorb so much. If change is too fast, then it creates chaos and fear.

> #20 *To try to create a multiple location quality program is unrealistic without the development of a corporate model.*

A Positive Note

The change in corporate culture must promote performance and stability without suggesting loss of identity. This is accomplished by the employees remembering the four barriers to quality through corporate leadership.

Bruce

WHAT'S NEXT

I bet you really didn't know how you were doing business— it comes as a shock to most companies. You've defined your structure, though, and that's over.

Next, take a look at your employees. Are they really ready to help you develop quality? do they have the necessary skills? Maybe they do—maybe they don't.

7
BASESKILLS OF EMPLOYEES

BASESKILLS DEFINED

The term *"BaseSkills"* will be used synonymously with the term *"basic skills."* The reason being is that BaseSkills are basic to the overall development of employees. I use the term "base" because I feel these skills provide a firm base from which you can build an organization with the environment that provides an employee with the opportunity to take pride in the triad of work, home, and self.

Why did I develop BaseSkills training? That's a fair question. The reason is once I started training within the organizations, Then I could see that many employees did not really have the BaseSkills that would help them through the process and the formal meetings. (I know what you're thinking—I haven't told you what the skills are. Keep reading!)

BaseSkills are how we look and present ourselves. They involve simple things like putting our head up and our shoulders back, shaking hands, presenting a positive image, and things like how we say hello and talk to one another. I felt a need to teach employees how to present themselves in a good, positive mode because I didn't want employees penalized "right out of the chute" based on the first impression made. I know from experience that within the first five seconds someone sees you, they form a personal opinion of you based on how you present yourself. The first impression is lasting..

Personal perception is one of the strongest things I try to get across to team members and employees. The fact is, whether you like it or not, people are forming an opinion and strengthening it every time they see you.

PERSONAL SEMINARS

Story #21

As we developed the organization's BaseWork Systems 2000, we began to believe that there was a great need for personal skills training. As a result, we developed what we call one-hour, one-page workshops. These were developed as we experienced the need for teaching employees basic skills regarding communication, planning, scheduling, problem-solving, task-teaming, and teamwork. We had taken for granted up front that employees had these skills.

After my experiences, I now have a firm belief that a lot of necessary skills for our society have not been taught. These include things such as communicating a point or a problem to somebody without getting upset or hostile. We feel in BaseWork Systems 2000 that, if we can teach and give interpersonal skills training, it is not only going to help the company, but it will help the family and community.

We have many stories coming back to us of how employees have taken the skills they have learned in class to their home environment and how it changed their lives. We believe that one day the general public will attend personal seminars much like those at work, but it will be a family project where the parents and children go together.

Our goal is to give this education to the masses in our country and beyond. By so doing, we hope to bring an awareness to even third world countries. Many people in those countries don't have the BaseSkills. Even though they're just as intelligent as anybody else, they haven't had the basic skill training.

The required knowledge base exists; it just isn't being communicated down to all levels of the population where it really needs to go. It is ludicrous to know how to solve issues or problems and not give that particular information to people in the marketplace.

I really believe we're going to create not only a set of complete basic seminars for an entire organization, but our system is also going to become the University of the Future and the basis for family training. We oftentimes go through life stumbling. Given the proper training, we wouldn't make many of the mistakes we do as individuals and companies wouldn't do a lot of the things they do.

Our goal at BSG International, Inc. is to get this education to the masses, and at a price that's affordable, so if they want it, they have access to it.

> #21 *Interpersonal skill awareness brings new life to an organization and the community.*

IMPORTANCE OF POSITIVE ATTITUDE

I constantly get arguments from employees on this subject. They say one should not judge who you are until they actually meet you. I couldn't agree more! Reality exists, however. The sad thing is that none of us get a second chance to make a first impression, especially if you're in sales. You may spend the time you do have with a customer trying to alter the negative impression created when you first met. You spend your selling time trying to justify the type person you are. Forget it—that person has already formulated an opinion and tuned you out. When you spend time trying to sell yourself instead of product, where's the profit in that?

It's very important that you present a good, positive image. If you're cognizant of how you're holding your head and shoulders, if you're smiling, and if you're looking like you are a positive leader—guess what. You become an upbeat, positive leader. Why? If you believe in yourself, you subconsciously convey confidence, and will project it.

If you appear positive and happy, people will give you the benefit of doubt and assume you're what you appear to be. That perception is very important at work and to your personal presentation. Additionally, you take the skill home and it reflects on how your kids and spouse perceive you to be. It's very important that you understand the informal communication that you're sending to the receiver.

Another area of concern was personal responsibility. As a result, I developed a workshop based on input received from employees.

WORKSHOPS

I have developed many workshops for employee training. I will discuss the following one as an example of the type training needed. It is a simple rendering of basic workshop content.

WORKSHOP ON PERSONAL RESPONSIBILITY

During the workshop, I try to impart that you have responsibilities whether you like it or not. One of the things that I ask in the introduction is, "Why do you think companies resist implementing programs of this quality?" The responses come back that it costs too much, it takes too much time, they don't care, and they don't think they need it. Then you ask questions of the team members.

- ◆ "What does **SMILE** mean?" You emphasize that the first half hour at work sets the tone for the rest of the day. You then discuss the meaning of the acronym, **SMILE**. You have the power to either be positive or negative—it is totally up to you and no one else. Let's work on being up and positive the first half hour at work each day.
- ◆ You ask employees about the three stages of their lives: the teen years (high school), the present (working years), and

retirement. During the first stage, you grow up and make friends. You then move to the present—your working years. Most people move from high school or college directly into the workforce. You are forced to grow up overnight—one day you're a student, the next day you have a job and a whole new set of responsibilities. The final step is retirement. You should stress the different needs, wants, and requirements of each stage. Employees need to understand that each level requires a different set of BaseSkills, or at least the application of BaseSkills in different ways.

♦ You ask them to name something that was happy or positive in the teen years. The response usually is that your families made you feel happy and positive in the teen years. Second influence was your friends. Third was your girl or boy friends. Fourth was that some people just lived for the day, and number five was sports.

♦ Why did you do something right or wrong in the teen years? The response will be varied. It was because it was fun. You wanted to fit in. You didn't really know any better, and you really weren't thinking about tomorrow— you were just living for the day.

♦ Are you still doing the same things as in the teen years? Most answer—no.

♦ Why do you think you've changed? Mainly because you got married and settled down, had children, and developed responsibilities. That's how most people move towards responsibility—getting married and having children.

♦ How many of you know someone that still hangs out like in the teen years? Almost all of you know someone that hasn't really grown up and is still doing the same things they were in high school.

♦ What makes most of you change? The answer is responsibility. One way or another, that makes you change. Maybe you've bought a car and now you're responsible for the payment and that forces you to become responsible. Or you've moved out of the house and are now paying rent. You are now responsible for those bills and others.

♦ What are the most important things in your life? The number one response is usually family, number two is children and providing a better life for them, and the third is work. If you look at it, most of you are concerned about your families and you all want to build something better for your children.

♦ How many of you think that your father and mother had the same concerns you do? You almost all believe that your parents thought the same as you do.

♦ Did most of you see as much of your fathers as you wanted to? The answer is mostly, no. When I ask why, most say they were working. Many of you grew up thinking that you were the only ones that missed your fathers. Whereas, after polling you discovered almost everyone had a feeling that their father was out working and you didn't spend as much time with him as you wanted. It didn't matter whether your income was poor, middle or upper.

♦ Where are you with your life? Slow down, think and plan. Step back, think, and plan your way through your life. The program's position is that there must be a balance between work and home life—if not, something will short-circuit somewhere.

♦ How do you spend your time? Half of your life revolves around work. Either going to, coming back from, or on the job. Sometimes you see more of your co-workers than your family. You think it's very important that you have a balance and that you learn to communicate with your co-workers and care about them. I use as an example that, after talking; do you not feel that you have the same thoughts and concerns as the other guy? All employees seem to have the same thoughts and concerns.

♦ Ask them to look around and understand that everyone is in this together. An example of what I've seen in many companies: sometimes you think you're the only one with problems— financial, marital, children, and health. What you try to do is make employees aware that they all have problems and that they need to be thinking about helping each other. Your family is getting feedback from you concerning what you're doing at work. It is very important that you put yourself in your family's shoes and understand that they perceive you as the leader of the household. You want everybody to see you're all in this together and have a lot in common.

♦ You need to develop support for employees. You are, in a sense, a family, and it's important to get along. Your goal is for the company to be a great, caring entity.

♦ One of the biggest problems that all of us have is time. How do you allocate such a precious commodity between family, friends, and yourselves. As you examine the issue, you'll find that as you get busy with life and living, you have fewer friends than you did in your teen years and you have less time. You've already talked about the fact that you spent over half of your waking hours at work, so you have very little time. You need to make time for family and friends, and you especially need to make time for yourself. You are working day in and day out and typically, you make time for everybody but yourselves.

♦ Can you be happy without balance between your work life and home life? My position is that you're going to spend time in the workshops learning how to be in control of your home life and work life. The company is committed to helping you balance the two because that is the origin of much workplace conflict.

♦ You need to manage time and to schedule both at work and at home. Even go so far as to plan your off days and schedule them. The importance of time management must be communicated with family and colleagues at work. For example, you talk about the plant being down for maintenance. If you don't schedule plant production time and you know that preventive maintenance will occur in month 6, day 4, and you don't plan, it then throws everybody's schedule off. By not scheduling the plant downtime, chaos can be the order of the day.

UNIVERSITIES OF TOMORROW

Story #22

After going into many companies and working with employees, I discovered a tremendous lack of base skills. These base skills include math, English, communication, self-worth, business administration, and parenting. When we teach these skills and I see employees taking what we teach them at work and applying it with great benefit to their home lives, it makes me think.

We have discovered that many children learn skills in school, but then lose them because the parents aren't trained to help them integrate these tools into their daily lives. We parents can train our children as much as possible, teachers can do the best they can do, but unless we model it for our children, there is a conflict.

At any given time there is only three to ten percent of the general population unemployed. That statistic means that the parents who need to be influencing their children are in the workforce.

If we are going to help society by giving to charity, then maybe we should pay attention to the old saying, "charity begins at home." Let's give it to our employees. Let's train our own employees.

That is the basis of the BaseWork Systems 2000. Not only will it help our business, but also our families, our community, and our country because employees will become all-around better people.

When our small children come home and say, "Let's be at peace with all people," the parents now have the understanding and the compassion to say, "You're right." They can now communicate and reinforce what the child is learning—because now they have base skills and the perception that if they don't act like good people, then they won't be perceived as good. That builds negatives against us and our families.

So, as companies, instead of giving to charity, give to your own people. If we have every company giving to their own employees, then we will reach the masses through education. There are the negative "bean counters" that worry about the cost of such an excellent program. If you look at the statistics that say 30 to 40% of the day is wasted by your average worker, then use some of that time for training. Two hours of training a month is the basis of my program. Why not gain back some of that time that was lost. The universities of tomorrow will be in our businesses and corporations.

Here is another thought for you. Without good company training programs, where will our immigrant labor force be? These are good people—are no different than the rest of us; they have good family values. Our immigrant Employees are wonderful, hard-working people. Several of these cultures remind me of the people in the south with close family ties and compassionate behavior.

It is our responsibility to train them; we have hired them and allowed and encouraged them to come into our country. Their lack of awareness is not their fault. If we are willing to give them direction, we will all benefit. That is why I believe that our companies will be the universities of tomorrow.

> #22 *Our organizations will become the universities of tomorrow with the employees being the students.*

There is a closing note. Do you know someone that always seems to have something wrong in his or her life? Someone did him wrong or a dark cloud is following him around and he always has an excuse for something not being his fault? Do you think that person ever stops and thinks that perhaps it's them—that he is his own worst enemy? How much of this has to do with him accepting responsibility for his own attitude?

The class will always agree. You're in control of your life—stay away from those negative people. Remember the two rules: 1) do what is morally and ethically correct, and 2) treat everybody as you want to be treated. Responsibility includes, whether you like it or not, the fact that most of you have to have a job in order to pay your bills.

SEVEN TO ONE POSITIVE

Story #23

People have a tendency to remember seven negatives to every one positive. That's why it is very important to take into account our own wins and never discount them. If we have a great day, we seem to say, "That's fine, but let's move on." Whereas, when we have a bad day we tend to dwell on the negatives

If you look at a movie, you will remember more of the negative events than the positive. What triggers this? Maybe we think that the positives have little impact—nothing will change or happen because of them. If it's a negative, however, we dwell on it because we fear it will happen to us. As workers, we always seem to focus on the negatives.

We need to turn this thinking around and have seven positive thoughts for every negative thought. If we're thinking in a positive vein, we become positive. As you're working you need to remember that. People won't remember how you looked the one day going into a client's office dressed nicely; they'll remember the "bad hair days," or times you were down in your demeanor or physical appearance.

We need to reinforce the positives in our lives and take account of our wins. Being positive helps flower the soul—it adds richness. Negative thoughts eat away at us like cancer. Don't forget that people will remember seven negatives to one positive. If we're in this program and are focusing on the negative things and don't see our positives, then we will be much less effective.

> #23 *A lesson learned from a negative experience is positive.*

In summarizing the workshop on responsibility:

1. You must let everyone know what the program is about. It is about moving and changing for the right reason.
2. You almost all share the same thoughts and concerns.
3. There needs to be a balance between home life and work life.
4. Job and quality of life are very important.
5. You have to step up to the responsibilities of your families and jobs.
6. You also have the responsibility for the success of the quality program—it is not just a management responsibility.
7. There are no excuses; you must accept the responsibility. If you have a problem, write a quality issue. Hold everyone accountable for quality without personal or group attacks.

The ball is now in your court. If this thing does not work, then you need to look at yourself in the mirror. You need to think, plan, schedule, and win. Remember, responsibility is the key to yourself, your family, and your job.

In closing, you're committed; you've been given a tool and hopefully, if you are having problems or concerns, you can step up and take the responsibility for making change. With any luck, you have been given the encouragement and the support to make it happen.

End of workshop example

SUMMARY

These BaseSkills were developed out of a need that employees had concerning basic interpersonal and communication skills as well as planning, scheduling and monitoring. It was very important that I write what I call my one-page, one-hour workshops. They were designed with a one-page hand-out so the employee could see the bullet points, talk about them, and take the hand-out home. Later, they could review and apply it.

I have seen employees coming back years later and saying that the problem-solving, communication, planning, and scheduling skills now help them in their home lives. They can communicate with their children, husbands and wives. Now they are scheduling their lives and it's not as chaotic. Things have slowed down and they've gotten their lives under control.

WHAT'S NEXT

By now, you are beginning to understand what the book title, BREAKING THROUGH THE 4 BARRIERS TO QUALITY, really means. Employee training in preparation for and as an integral part of—the quality process is obviously critical. Let's assume your employees are now ready to embark upon their quest for quality—what's next?

Next, you must help your employees develop a better understanding of their individual jobs; you must teach them how to define their jobs (I call this their BaseWork Center).

8

DEFINING YOUR JOB: THE BASEWORK CENTER CONCEPT

One of the interesting things that I found in my study of quality was that the majority (98%) of the problems in an organization are due to the four barriers to quality.

When I look at implied procedure, I feel that management is totally responsible for the systems or lack of systems internally within an organization. In order to formalize the way you are doing business and build business infrastructure, you must have the direction and commitment of management.

What I feel has been lacking in the training industry is a "how to" method for building business infrastructure. A lot of programs talk about what you should be doing but don't tell you how. BaseWork Systems 2000 not only tells you what you should be doing—it explains and shows you how to do it.

The systems are the way you do everything within the organization from manufacturing of the product/service to delivery, pick-up, and sales. If you can define your systems, document them, and have the procedures written by the people that do the jobs, whatever external problems you have will go away. The BaseWork Center (BW/C) concept is the foundation of the program. The system cannot be corrected or improved without first being defined by everyone involved.

All employees in the organization have a BaseWork Center. That is the foundation of their job. They are held accountable for everything in that BaseWork Center. Nothing else matters other than each person being held accountable for *their* BaseWork Center, process, steps and procedures. All employees involved in the process must define it and come to an agreement on the process, steps and procedures. Everyone that is involved in the job should be involved in the decision-making process.

WELDER'S PROBLEM

Story #24

As I started to get involved in these quality programs, I found a lot of things that just didn't make sense to me. I began going around to old clients and business associates and asking them about their quality programs.

One day I was participating in a problem-solving employee involvement meeting where we were brainstorming for problems. This company had been in the quality program for several years.

The team leader-coordinator started the meeting and asked if anyone had any problems to talk about. They went around the room and no one seemed to have anything to say. Then the coordinator asked if anyone had a complaint and a few people spoke up.

There was a big, gruff-looking welder sitting with his arms crossed. He had been with the company for 15 or 20 years and he seemed like a real sharp guy. He spoke up and admitted he had a problem. He stated that, whenever he got the blueprints from engineering, they were incorrect.

He explained that, when he would go over and try to talk to engineering to get them changed, engineering just raised hell and wouldn't do a thing. The coordinator asked what he did with the wrong blueprints, and the welder replied that he would just build it correctly.

"But," the welder said, "they weren't addressing the real issue that the blueprints needed to be changed."

The welder was very frustrated. The coordinator of the meeting jumped on him and told him that engineering wasn't his area of expertise. That was the engineer's department and problem. He told the welder his job was to weld and the engineer's job was to plan.

The coordinator said, "If that's the way they plan it, then build it that way."

By now, the welder was getting more and more frustrated and stated **that** type of thinking was wrong. The coordinator restated that engineering was not the welder's area of expertise. He had now gotten a little aggressive with the welder.

At that point, we lost the welder. He crossed his arms and literally shut down.

The coordinator continued with the meeting and asked if there were any other problems. He knew he had been a little rough on the welder. Since the welder was one of the best team members, the coordinator addressed the question to him, asking if he had any other problems.

The welder just looked at everyone in the room and said, "Yeah, we need bigger trash can liners."

This particular incident with the welder really brought a lot of things into focus. It gave me insight and caused me to question the way some quality programs were being run, especially in relation to their existing format and rules.

Over the last three to four years this company has sunk nearly 2 million dollars into their quality program. With most quality programs, it is stated that you should be in the same meeting with the people that do the same types of jobs. You should focus on areas that you can control or that you're responsible for.

The welder story is a perfect example, demonstrating that many things with which companies have problems are really happening in what I call other BaseWork Centers. These are activities that affect them either directly or indirectly. My position is that these activities must be addressed. If the employee feels it's a problem, then it must be addressed.

In my program, I designed Four Problem-Solving Processes. Process A is the Five Step: brainstorming for problems. Process B is Task Team Format: this task team format states that if you have a problem, you can form a task team of individuals outside your

BaseWork Center. Typically, these individuals are also affected by the particular problem.

Take the welder for example. He can form a task team with whoever is involved in the process of the incorrect blueprints. This allows the welder, the engineers, the person who gives the specs to the engineer, and whoever else is involved in processing those blueprints to get together and address the problem.

Through the Task Team Format, my program is designed to address this type of BaseWork Center issue. Most other quality programs don't allow for this type of regularly occurring situation.

I also found that other programs just start brainstorming on problems, interpreting problems the way they perceive them. They weren't really looking in any particular direction, because everybody's interpretation of quality is different.

So, here's a company that has spent three to four years in a two million dollar quality program and their employees are brainstorming that they need bigger trash can liners.

I asked the welder if he had ever been taught what a quality system is, or what the company wants him to look for in the way of improvements. His answer was no—they had just started brainstorming for problems.

I asked the welder if he had ever defined his job. He didn't know what I meant. So I asked if he had ever written what we call a BaseWork Center, or defined his job or procedures in writing. He said no.

It amazed me that this company has been in the quality program for that length of time, has real issues, and yet can't address them because they haven't defined how they are doing business. My program's position is that you can't improve a system or process until you define it. Yet, here is a coordinator in a meeting looking for problems when the employees haven't defined their BaseWork Center.

This is a great example that led me to build into my program a way to help the teams be productive from day one. Most of the problem-solving programs or brainstorming programs are not productive.

The employees have no idea the direction the company wants them to go.

My system is a totally directed quality program: meaning we know where we're going, and how we're going to get there; we know what we are going to do, and what our end results will be. I can give these employees direction from the beginning because once they start defining their job or systems, that definition starts clarifying and getting rid of problems.

I also teach the employees about truly understanding their jobs. I am talking about their BaseWork Center, which includes all the job's processes, steps and procedures. The systems and processes now make sense when the job is defined in a written format.

The welder's problem could have been addressed as a quality issue. The quality issues could have dealt with an engineer who was disinterested when the welder brought the problem to her—the problem being that this employee/welder believed the system was incorrect regarding the blueprints.

Within my program, the welder would also have the option of forming a Task Team. This example shows that the welder's company did not have the tools to fix and address these problems.

> #24 *Frustration is knowing the solution to the problem, yet not possessing the responsibility nor trust to resolve it.*

THE JOB

Each job has process(es) and steps, with the processes linked internally by the suppliers and customers who make up the systems. Most of the problems with external customers and suppliers are due to lack of systems internally. By defining the internal system, which you can control, the external problems then become manageable. System by system the external and internal problems vanish.

Just think what makes an unhappy customer. It's usually something that's been done internally. Oftentimes, it is poor quality in either the product or service or both. The goal is to have quality that can be defined, monitored, and continuously improved! Management cannot do this alone. Not only do they need the tool, but they must have the involvement of every employee in the organization and every BaseWork Center.

As you define the BaseWork Center, the packet will bring into agreement all employees doing the same job. The process and steps define what you do, the steps in which you do them, and the written procedure for doing them. Remember, think of the process(es) of your BaseWork Center and the steps within the process.

Oftentimes, you find people doing their jobs and thinking, "Boy, this sure isn't what I was hired to do." Once you start working through why the person was hired, his main area of expertise and control, and his responsibility, then you'll find that a lot of people internally in the company have the same BaseWork Center. What has happened, because of the lack of infrastructure, is that things are implied as to who is doing what.

Take for example, Warehousemen. If you ask two of them to describe their jobs and process, they may believe they have different jobs. They need to agree on the process and steps, even if you have three shifts. The process and steps should be the same, with a few additional duties that change. Perhaps in the evening, because you aren't shipping and receiving, more emphasis is put on the paperwork. That could be additional duties performed daily, weekly and monthly, and as needed. It is the same shipping and receiving job, but the priorities are different and daily duties have a little different focus. Basically, though, the job is the same.

WAREHOUSE JOB

Story #25

In one of the companies where we worked, they had two warehouse men. In talking to them about their BaseWork Centers and asking for a job description, they appeared to have two completely different jobs.

One person was shipping and the other person was receiving. Their jobs overlapped, but neither really understood both the shipping and the receiving. They were both just doing the best they could.

One of the problems that cropped up proved to be a good basis for our BaseWork Center component called Additional Duties. It involved the point at which the truck driver pulled up to have his truck unloaded. The truck driver would see the man on the forklift (the receiver) taking tires out of inventory and putting them into stock. The implied procedure is that if the warehouse person is there, then he is to help the driver unload his truck. The driver got upset because when he would pull up, the receiver was never available to help. We have two people who thought they were doing what was correct and working hard but are frustrated with the situation.

The company had to make a decision concerning which was more important taking tires out of inventory, or unloading the truck and getting it back out on the street. Everyone's idea of what was most important was different. This is where we felt it necessary to organize the BaseWork Centers to include Additional Duties that were accomplished daily, weekly, monthly, and as needed.

This particular BaseWork Center covered all duties starting with receiving and going all the way to shipping. The decision was made that we wanted one job, not two different jobs. Maybe the man in shipping did steps ll through 22 and the guy in receiving did 1-10. That's fine, but it was still considered one job. There had to be cross-training to understand both sides. The main purpose of both people was to do shipping **and** receiving.

What we found was that the trucks stayed in an hour or two longer than necessary. We needed to have them unloaded and back out on route.

After we sat down and talked to everybody, we saw that the warehouse man was getting pressure from manufacturing to move the product out and into inventory. From the overall company perspective, however, the main priority of that job was to unload the truck. The warehouse man could put inventory in anytime.

We also found that there were time discrepancies with these jobs, noticing that the warehouse men got in several hours before there was anything to do. We asked why they were coming in early, and they couldn't answer that. In defining the job, we changed their hours to more closely coincide with need, thus, making the whole operation more efficient. Before the change, they were coming in several hours before the work actually started and were leaving before the trucks were unloaded. Also, prior to the change, they were not fulfilling the needs of their internal customers and suppliers.

By working through the BaseWork Center, things began to run much smoother and it eased the friction between these BaseWork Center employees. There was no longer a need to point fingers and people were no longer being blamed for not doing the job correctly. In fact, everyone was busy doing what they interpreted to be a matter of priority and what management wanted them to do.

You can't blame the employees for the previous situation—the BaseWork Center had not been defined. They now agree on the processes, steps and additional duties, whether daily, weekly, monthly, or as needed.

> #25 *In an informal organization, the job priority is the priority of the day.*

Remember, one of the biggest problems for business is training; you can't train until you have written procedures, and you can't get those until you have the people that are doing the job define the procedure in their own terminology. In order to get them to define the job, they have to believe it is what management wants.

BASEWORK CENTER DEVELOPMENT

In the beginning, I stumbled around a bit in the definition of jobs. First, I began to ask for certain things back in regard to employees' jobs. I began getting all kinds of information back, most of it useless. Employees couldn't figure out what was their BaseWork Center. They kind of knew what their job was, but it was constantly changing.

In response to the confusion, I created what I call a "Summary of Forms/Paperwork" form that tells us exactly what forms and paperwork pass through a particular BaseWork Center. Employees were asked to list paperwork by form name including any form reference number.

Additional information requested was the originator and to whom they pass it. The paperwork usually suggests a process and the steps of the BaseWork Center. Paperwork is a good way to get started in organizing your thoughts in the BaseWork Center.

The next thing I did was ask each employee to list all the things they did in the company. They did this on a worksheet called "Defining BW/C." I wanted them to list every little thing they did. I found that they became very realistic in writing this information down. One of the problems, however, was fear. They were afraid that if they didn't put down enough, their job might be in jeopardy because deep down each employee felt they could be replaced. Or, they felt someone could come in and do the job for less money. Those were the fears that surfaced.

After the employee listed his or her duties, I asked them to go back and mark whether the duties were performed daily, weekly, monthly, other, or as needed. Now I had a list of the forms and job duties, which helped me organize. The paperwork began to formalize the

BaseWork Center. Usually, when I talk about doing something daily, it's more likely the basis of the BaseWork Center. As you sort through it, you agree on your process and steps. You then see the additional duties—daily, weekly, monthly, and as needed.

You also need to define the terms for every BaseWork Center. You ask the employees to state what their job and title is. That tells you what their main responsibility is and what their title is (or what they think their job/title is).

Then you ask them to list what product or service they provide. What is it that they are doing for the company in their BaseWork Center? What is the main focus of their job? You wouldn't believe how difficult this is for them to figure out.

You then assign a BaseWork Center number for reference purposes. The first two numbers are the division, the next four are department, and the next two are the job within that department. Using this number, you can track the procedures and additional duties—daily, weekly, and monthly. List all the employees in the company that have the same BaseWork Center on the form.

Also, ask the employees to list *to whom* they report at the first, second, and third levels. Don't ask them to list the boss, but instead list the person they interact with daily for work assignments. One not so surprising thing you see happen is that everybody thinks he reports to the President of the company. That in itself creates conflict; you would not believe how much trouble it stirs up. That is why you need to go in and define the corporate organizational structure first thing.

GRIPEITIS

Story #26

One of the most devastating things in a company is what I call gripeitis. It always seems to start with the negative one percent who always seem to be complaining.

Gripeitis takes many forms. It takes form in verbal complaints and attitude. It takes form in a company's health and welfare. No matter what happens or how good things are going, some people are going to find the negative and complain about it. For example, we had one employee I remember when we first started my program. I walked through the door and a man came up to me and said, "You look awful. It looks like you've got cancer. You ought to shoot yourself." I found out this employee had been there many years and was very negative.

As the program went on, we found that in his particular BaseWork Center, there was a lot of negativism and a lot of absenteeism and tardiness. Mr. Negative in particular had high absenteeism and tardiness. When we talked to him about his BaseWork Center, his comment was that he reported to the owner of the company. It was quite obvious he was not being held accountable for anything.

Everyone walked on pins and needles around this guy. Nobody knew exactly what he did. He held the company hostage. When the meetings were in full swing, he always had a great excuse to miss and was always going from one fire to another.

Gripeitis puts a negative slant on everything that happens. There was never anything that went right. There was always something negative. He never said anything positive. Everyone in that BaseWork Center took on the same negative rap.

Finally, the guy retired. You would not believe how the mood in that one department changed when he left. It was as different as night and day. When we talked about being happy in the morning and **SMILE**, doing the right thing, and caring for one another—he was the first to be negative. But he was also the first one to call it quits.

I started thinking about all the negative energy that had been in that one department for over 15 years. Just think how inefficient that was. Where do you look on a balance sheet to see what **that** cost? It's hard to put a dollar amount on what that cost the company. Just think of the employees that one man drove away, the customers he drove away, the bad deals made, and the hidden agendas. All this was the company's fault because they let him get away with it. He never had a positive thought. That's why "gripeitis" is contagious. You get one group or even one person and it spreads like an out-of-control disease. One person starts and thinks it is acceptable to grip and complain. They never promote positive feelings and never give a pat on the back because, for whatever reason, this is how they operate.

"Gripeitis" eats away at the BaseValues in an organization. I can guarantee you that a person, like the aforementioned, has problems at home, too. This particular guy sure did; he had been married four times.

> #26 *Stay away from the negative person because he will suck the life, breath and enthusiasm out of you and your organization.*

PROCESSES AND STEPS

The next thing you do is look at your BaseWork Center, area of expertise or control, your job, and list all the additional duties—daily, weekly, monthly, and as needed. You also list Process and Steps, very specifically. You don't just say you start the machine; you say there are two steps. Don't combine the steps. For example, I start up the machinery. What do you do when you first start it? You turn the key on to start the ignition. Next, you hit the control panel "C". That is two steps instead of just saying you start the machine. List **all** the steps in the process.

Once you list the steps, you have defined your process and steps. Next, go over it with your managers and fellow team members. Sometimes, that takes a week or even a month or so to go through because you'll find that everyone is doing it differently. The company has to come to an agreement about the most efficient set of steps for accomplishing the process. For example, you had one company where the trucks were going out and doing a particular function at the end of the day. According to the Department of Transportation procedures, they were out of sync with the required procedures, so you had to make sure they were not only doing what management wanted, but what was required by law.

ADDITIONAL DUTIES

The next step is defining the duties, job priorities, and additional duties and information. You look at everything you listed and make sure it is slotted somewhere. Then, for your BaseWork Center you look at your internal suppliers and customers—who you receive your work from and give it to internally. Also, consider external suppliers and customer—who the company gets your supplies from and who are external customers. Also during the team meeting, you want them to define their mission statement and their goals for the particular BaseWork Center.

Now that you have defined the BaseWork Center package, you want to make sure you are able to manage the information. You need to establish information centers where all the information will be kept.

PROCEDURE DEVELOPMENT

You need to look at your thought process for developing a procedure. What is done? When is it done? Under what circumstances is it done? Who does it? Where is it done? What resources (material, tools, equipment) are needed? Where are those resources kept? Why is it done? For each step of that process there will be a written procedure and that will define how you do that step. You have to define the procedure. Now you need to list it by BaseWork Center Number. Every employee that is involved with that particular procedure should get a copy of it for inclusion in the BaseWork Center packet.

Now, step back and look at what has been done. You have developed your BaseWork Center, your process, steps, and procedures for what you are held accountable, you have additional duties—daily, weekly, monthly, and as needed, and you have procedures, written and agreed upon by the people that do the jobs. When you link all these processes and the paperwork together, you create the systems within the organization.

SUMMARY

In summary, the BW/C procedure probably started communication, sometimes for the first time, between employees and employees, and between employees and management, because everyone had to work together to reach a consensus agreement. Remember, no one person can kill the deal; it has to be the agreement of all the people doing the job.

Some middle and upper management may resist, saying the employees are going to run wild. What I've experienced is that the employees are going to hold themselves and their teammates more accountable than management could ever hope. As long as there are no hidden agendas, the employees are going to do a good job.

When you look at the BaseWork Centers, you will have to come to agreements and make tough decisions. The tough decisions are defining what the BaseWork Center is and deciding to hold everybody accountable. That's how you stop non-quality —dead in it's tracks. You don't accept or pass on non-quality.

Once you've defined what your internal customers and suppliers require and your process and steps, you now know what is expected. You no longer pass it on if it's not correct. That eliminates the need for final inspectors. Everyone, in their own BaseWork Center, should be their own final inspector. That is the key to building business infrastructure in an organization. What you are doing is formalizing the way you're doing business, formalizing your thoughts, and writing them down.

Watch out for hearsay and "what-ifs"; they can slow down the process. Implement this information correctly and you'll discover that the employees will do a very good job with the BaseWork Center concept.

OUT-SOURCING BASE WORK CENTERS

Story #27

We, as a country, have gotten into what I consider a bad habit—out-sourcing. In America today, we out-source everything from janitorial services to human resource management. Some of it is justified, especially as we get more global; some of it is not. For example, we cannot compete with the 67-cent-a-day labor in China. Even at 100% efficiency, we will never compete with that.

As we start looking at out-sourcing, one of our problems is that we have never taken the time to define what we are out-sourcing; we don't define BaseWork Centers. We don't really understand the jobs and procedures well enough to out-source with any comfortable degree of efficiency.

What is out-sourcing doing to employees? Many may be staying at home and working on the computer without having to travel to the office. We all know the benefits of that—or do we?

The big problem is that we haven't really defined the job or procedure of that particular BaseWork Center/job. What exactly is it that the employee is supposed to be doing at home?

The thing I dislike about out-sourcing is that we are not comparing apples with apples. For example, let's look at our larger manufacturers in this country. The corporate directive is to cut expenses 10%. Remember, it's easier to cut expenses than change the process. There is no tool in place to improve the process. So, we put it out to bid. If we tell them our number is x, and we have to beat x, y, and z, they will come up with that number. Many may actually take a loss or nearly no profit. To do that, the successful bidder's employees will ultimately pay the price.

We need to set an example for our employees. We have to make a decision. Are we going to out-source to a company that pays less and has no benefits? Are we doing what is morally and ethically correct for their employees? When we are out-sourcing, we can't look at it as a way to cut cost, but rather as a way of improving the way we do business. If we improve internally, we will bring our cost down and become more competitive. If we out-source, we'll have a better idea of what we're expecting and we will be holding ourselves and others accountable for quality.

Quality will not cost jobs but will create jobs. Let's not look at cutting employees and cutting expenses because we're inefficient. We have a responsibility to our employees so let's look at how we can improve business.

We need to be careful of out-sourcing. We have a social responsibility, whether we like it or not. We can look at the pension funds and use a typical Teacher's Association as an example. They have to hold that pension fund advisor accountable—to make right and wise investments in companies that are socially responsible, not only to their employees but to the country and what we stand for.

> *#27* *An organization has to be socially responsible to its employees, community and country in both its short and long-term thinking. If a company is socially responsible and committed to its employees, then it will meet the needs of the community and the country.*

BaseWork Centers
Worksheet

A) Department: What Product or Service Do We Provide?

BW/C # _____ Team # _____

BW/C NAME _____

B)   Team Member   C) BW/C Process/Steps

1. _____   1. _____
2. _____   2. _____
3. _____   3. _____
4. _____   4. _____
5. _____   5. _____
6. _____   6. _____

D)   Suppliers - External   7. _____
_____   8. _____
_____   9. _____
_____   10. _____
_____   11. _____

     Suppliers - Internal   12. _____
_____   13. _____
_____   14. _____
_____   15. _____

E)   Customers - Internal   Customers - External
_____   _____
_____   _____
_____   _____

F)   Quality Goals: _____
_____
_____

G)   Quality Statement: _____
_____
_____

WHAT'S NEXT

As you have no doubt realized at this juncture in your reading, BaseWork Centers and their definition are at the heart of developing quality in your company. They are also an integral part of the next thing I want to talk about.

Next, I want to explain systems and their overall importance to the company. Because BaseWork Centers are critical to understanding systems, I explained them first. As the explanation of systems progresses, I will revisit some of the information covered in the previous chapter, so that you can understand it in the context of systems.

Have you figured out the method to my madness yet? Basically, I want you to understand the four barriers to quality and how change can start to break them down; I want you to understand how you are currently doing business and the incumbent problems; I want you to understand the necessity for employee preparation and buy-in to the quality process; I want you to understand the importance of employee job definition; and next, I want you to understand there must be a systemic connection between individual jobs. The connecting jobs equal systems.

9

DEFINING ORGANIZATIONAL SYSTEMS

A *system* is the way we do things in an organization; it is usually made up of processes, steps, and procedures. When they are joined together by internal customers/suppliers, the combination creates systems. All we're doing is flowcharting the systems. When the employee looks at her paperwork, it will usually suggest a process and/or a system.

Much of quality is trying to figure out what the terminology is and what we're talking about. From our definition, we know that a process is a particular method of doing something, usually involving a number of steps or operations. A system is a set of processes arranged in a regular, orderly form and linked together. Process(es) equals system: each team member (employee) has a BaseWork Center or a job. That job has a process consisting of several steps. After defining the process and steps, the employee then writes procedures for those steps.

System = Internal Suppliers + BaseWork Center + Internal Customers
BaseWork Center = One or More Processes
Process = Step(s) + Written Procedure(s)

Employees receive work from their internal supplier. After completing the process and steps, they give it to their internal customer. Between the time of receiving and the time of giving, gaps can occur. Those are system gaps where many things can happen.

- ➢ What employees want is usually different from what they are getting and giving to their internal supplier/customers. This simply comes from lack of communication, written procedures, and training.
- ➢ Things are lost/misplaced.
- ➢ Products are damaged or handled twice.
- ➢ Paperwork problems such as lack of, lost or insufficient paperwork surfaces.

A good system comes not from inspection, but from the improvement of processes, steps and procedures that make up the systems. You should not inspect bad quality out, but instead build good quality into the system.

From a system approach, you are either selling a **product** or **service** or both. Remember, there are exceptions to every rule. My definition of a product is something that is produced or manufactured. A service is a product of human activity to satisfy a need. Examples of a product are things that are produced or manufactured (tangible). A service is intangible—although just as valuable as a product; it cannot be picked up or felt.

When you manufacture a widget **product**, the delivery of the widget by your driver is the **service.** Note that most manufacturing companies deal with systems made of processes, steps and procedures for what is produced. Service companies' systems are made up of processes, steps and procedures for the paperwork dealing with the sale/service. Most organizations have a combination of both product and service with which to deal.

How do you determine what a system is, if you want to improve it, if you want to work on it, or define it? Because there is lack of formalization in most organizations, you want to look at how you go about determining what a system is. Typically, a system is the joining of processes, steps, and procedures.

If you want to identify an employee's BaseWork Center, or the particular system or process for which they are responsible, then you must start by listing the paperwork, the forms, and the reports that they're completing. By collecting the paperwork, it will suggest a system.

SYSTEMS

Story #28

My program feels that system problems within an organization are due to lack of communication (verbal and written) and/or implied procedures. These problems are due to lack of written procedures that define that system.

We try to look at and define a system. By this we mean the way we do things internally within an organization. This may involve filling out a Purchase Order, shipping, receiving, accounts payable and receivable, purchasing, manufacturing, or production. Everything in an organization is a system.

We were confronted early on with how to improve these systems and how to break them down? There are so many jobs within a company and so many systems. We took a straightforward look at the company and developed BaseWork Centers, processes, and steps.

Look at the manufacturing of a product. The raw materials come in, go through a number of manufacturing steps, come out as a finished product, and then are shipped. Looking at that system, you see it as very complex. We see it as different jobs and processes within that system.

The system is broken down by processes or BaseWork Centers. If you look at your organizational chart, you might use operators as an example. There may be six different process operators. Each process is different.

What we do is get that particular operator to look at the process within the BaseWork Center. He defines his process, steps, and procedures. When you connect the processes together by internal customer and supplier to whom I give my work and receive it from—that links the processes together, thus making up the system.

In order to attack these complex systems in an organization, we may send a manager out and tell him to fix the process. She wouldn't know where to begin. That manager tries to do it all and there is literally no way she can. The companies that try, fail. They can't problem-solve in this way.

A system defines the way we do everything within the organization. To break that system down requires identifying processes and people associated with processes. If several people touch the process, then we seek the person that owns it. For example, even though everyone in the company uses a purchase order, there is someone that is responsible for that purchase order in accounting. That person owns the process of the purchase order in accounting. We have to define who the person is that is responsible for that particular process, system or procedure. Most companies have a combination of warehousing, manufacturing, shipping, receiving, service, and other corporate structures. Everything will suggest a process and a step. That is how we look at a system within a company.

> #28 *No system is too complex when the people doing the actual job take it apart process by process, step by step and procedure by procedure.*

DEFINING THE PROCESS

Creating a flowchart should be your next step. Identify and sequence the process and its steps, examine it and define the procedure for each of the processes and steps. The key is to define it as the system exists. As you write and talk about it, you'll see a lot of things you can improve on immediately. But first, write it down and document it as it is. Then, if you have to go through a series of task teams *(see Chapter 10)*, then you can go through a proposed system, or system review.

Another important step is to determine who is monitoring the process or step. Look for the person who is monitoring the system, reviewing, processing, and reporting the data. You must determine who is accountable for that particular procedure and where it originated.

Let's say you've identified a particular system or process and the person/work area from whom you received it. When you receive the work from your internal supplier, how do you go about completing the process? That enumerates the steps in the process. You then need to list the steps. In doing that you will define the process and its steps—now go back and write those procedures into the formal process and steps.

DEFINING PROCEDURES

The problem with most procedures or operating manuals on the market is that the employee using the material had no input in writing the procedures. Another issue is that it is not in the employee's terminology, or the material is vague. It's very important to get the employees involved in defining the procedures. Why? Because the best person to develop material is the person who owns that procedure and uses it day in and day out.

DUST-COLLECTING MANUALS

Story #29

Most quality programs have some structure, program or operating procedure. Whether good or bad, most have huge manuals that end up sitting in the bookcase collecting dust. Companies will buy a canned procedure program that has to do with safety or some other concern. Even though it is vague and not necessarily applicable to their situation, they buy it anyway because it is internationally certified or something similar. That approach means the employees are never involved, because professional writers came in and certified the procedures and processes. The end result is a set of operating procedures sitting on a shelf out of reach for the people who have to implement them.

My program discusses breaking through the four barriers to quality by keeping information in front of employees, training and cross-training, communicating information, and utilizing employees to create written procedures. Manuals should be broken down by BaseWork Center and give employees training to define the BaseWork Centers around processes and steps.

Employees need to write the procedures with assistance from the people involved in the specific BaseWork Centers. Then they will have their written job description—along with their Team Member Handbook—with them at all times. That gives them immediate access to the information, thus, replacing the aforementioned dust-collecting manual.

There is a master file, but the file is broken down by jobs allowing it to become a vital tool for training and cross-training. Employees have the information in front of them everyday, so that it can be used for problem-solving or in case someone is out sick. Management can also refer to the master file to design training for additional departments.

By breaking the operating file down to BaseWork Centers, the information is less intimidating to the work force. Employees can easily access the information. Now everyone in the company is within arms reach of their operating procedures or BaseWork Centers. Instead of having to search through laborious manuals, every employee will have the procedure that applies to their job right in their hands.

Most training manuals are technical. For example, you will discover that most processes have been written by the engineer and/or technician that designed the process. Employees then have to determine what the engineers are talking about. By the time it gets on the work floor, it may be different all together.

For a written procedure to be used as a training tool, the employee that is doing the job on a daily basis must have a responsibility in defining the procedure. Trying to train out of technical manuals typically does not work very well. For the training to be truly effective, it should be monitored by incumbent employees using self-developed written procedures.

> #29 *If an employee is to have a manual about his BaseWork Center with accurate processes, steps, procedures and additional duties, the manual needs to be written by the employee.*

MEASURING AND GOAL SETTING

Next, define the steps in that process by developing procedures. That will give you the process and written steps on which employees have agreed.

Now, you can start to work on measuring and goal setting. You must first agree on what you are trying to accomplish and a mechanism for measuring the results. Most of the time this will improve productivity. It may be the first time that management and employees have understood what was needed and wanted by both in regard to production. Once you've collected that data, you can now set goals based on real data.

The most important thing is to get people involved in the data collection and goal setting and lead them through the process. If your organization seeks to improve productivity, you must find ways to measure the results. All goals must be realistic. There is nothing more insulting than unrealistic expectations and goals. If, for example, you've gotten into the game of asking for 15% more from the employees, employees know that's impossible.

You need to realistically look at where you want to be. At what level will the company make a reasonable profit? Start from there, and that, in turn will help inform the employees. Share with them the cost of the particular process, steps, and procedures, so they can start associating money, expense, and cost with their job. They then get a true understanding of why things can and can't be done in their particular job or department.

Determine what it is that your company is measuring: units, defects, etc. The time frame for which you are measuring should be a complete cycle that will best represent a true picture of what is being measured. The data collected that is above average will start to show in the Upper Control Limits (UCL). **Note: To start the process, use a measurement or specification of what is acceptable and not acceptable.**

After data collection, develop a measurement of what is average. This is also a good time to use break-even numbers (get the numbers from accounting) and then project a rate of return. This must be an honest number. Averaging is also a good goal setting tool. The Lower Control Limits (LCL) is the same as the UCL, but you are looking at the lower numbers. The key is not to make this any more complicated than it is!

Let's go through some examples of things to be measured.

- **Production Run:** Raw materials production, labor expense, defects per unit/per shift breakdown.
- **Trucking:** Pick-up, delivery, breakage, spillage, back tracking, expenses.
- **Absence/Tardiness:** Daily—excused, unexcused.
- **Office Workers:** Paperwork handled, time schedules, deadlines, A/P & A/R 30, 60, 90 terms.
- **Garage:** Parts delay, out of stock, hours billed, outside vendors (repair), inventory, outdated, balance, jobs not completed, maintenance, late/incomplete paperwork.
- **Maintenance**: Breakdowns, out of parts/inventory, jobs and hours logged, complete/incomplete paperwork.
- **Inventory:** Levels, dollar amount, problems.
- **Service:** Invalid sales order, unauthorized changes, rework, bad service, out of specification, customer not happy with our product or service.
- **Add to the List:** Your organization's thoughts.

The definition of a Control Chart is plotting (or charting) the potential results of what is measured. The easiest way of doing that is with a bar graph. You plot and measure the data collection. One of the best ways to introduce employees to control charts is to chart something that is common to all employees or to a particular BaseWork Center. Example, Start Up: charting and measuring what you are doing.

- ➢ **By: BaseWork Center**, Department, Division, Product/Service.
- ➢ **Absence/Tardiness:** Daily excused, unexcused, tardy.
- ➢ **Redo's/Waste/Scrap:** Production, service, delivery/ pick-up, and paperwork.
- ➢ **Cost of Down-Time:** Production, vehicles, paperwork.
- ➢ **Overtime:** Planned, unplanned.
- ➢ **Orders Handled:** How many?

➢ **Events:** Planned, unplanned during the day—events handled—"Putting out fires."

➢ **Data Collected:** Formal, informal, written, unwritten, bad forms, improved forms.

➢ **Inventory:** High, low, dollar, run outs.

➢ **Time:** To perform task, jobs, production, etc.

➢ **Customer Call-Ins:** Happy, unhappy, reasons.

➢ **Receipt of:** Defective products from vendors.

A STAKE IN THE GROUND

What do you do with data collected? When a process is under statistical control, its performance is more predictable. That is what you call your starting point—drive the stake in the ground and begin! You want to remove special causes regarding things that are not normal in an everyday production run. You want to make sure the data runs represent a normal run or a good cycle. Data has to be correct—good data going in, good data going out. You improve the process with data and you can set goals. You can't improve anything until you define how you're doing business in regard to process, steps, procedures, and system.

Once you've got everything in a controlled state and have formalized the process, steps, procedures, and systems in your business, you can now ***forever*** improve the product/service and process/system.

QUALIFY AND MONITOR

Story #30

What are we talking about here; what do qualify and monitor mean? When we talk about qualifying something, we mean to qualify data and also to qualify any questions asked. For example, I tell someone I need a product next week. They respond that they believe they can get it next week. I respond back, "Tell me when exactly you can deliver that product." If they come back and say they think they can deliver on Wednesday, then I need to qualify that and respond, "What time on Wednesday? We have to ship out by 6:00 p.m. Will it be ready by then?" They may respond, "I'll try."

You will find that a lot of people are uncomfortable with specifics about how things are going to happen, especially if they are being held accountable. It isn't because they don't want to be held accountable; it is because they are used to spending their days dealing with all kinds of fires and chaos within the organization. Flexibility has become their safety net over the years. They leave their day as flexible as they can because there's always something happening in the company to throw them off of their "unscheduled schedule." In the employees' defense, they have never had any real base management training on things such as scheduling, reporting, and planning. It's also very unusual for companies to stress accountability and holding individuals responsible. You can see this from our last example. There was a possibility of Wednesday—but then what time? They were evasive.

We have to be able to get back to our external or internal customer about the particular order, so we need to make sure we have quality and qualified information. Let's say we've agreed on the fact that we will get the product by 5:00 p.m. on Wednesday afternoon to meet our shipping deadline of 6:00 p.m. Now, what we need to do is follow up on it. If we don't monitor it, then we are leaving it to chance that the deal will come off. If you monitor it you are on top of the situation.

What we don't want to happen is that this conversation has taken place the week before that we don't ever call the manufacturer or our manufacturing department and follow up. Remember, our customer is planning on that particular product. To ensure they get it, we must monitor the entire process.

Monitoring requires determining what a reasonable time to follow up is. Set a schedule in your mind: in two days it should be in manufacturing. This way you can properly monitor the process. When you are monitoring and they say they've got it, don't stop there. You need to communicate with the shipper that it's a priority. Because, again, the shipping department has their way of doing business; they may decide other orders are more important, so they'll send ours out tomorrow. To make sure that we can live up to the dates we've been given, we must communicate and qualify information with everyone involved in the process.

When talking about good quality data, we qualify and we monitor the process all the way through. In a good quality program, everyone is held accountable for monitoring each other's process and for holding one another accountable. Until that happens, we have to take some over-cautious steps to make sure that what we've agreed on actually happens. Follow up is very important to monitoring. If we have agreed upon operating procedures or policies of procedure, then you have to monitor/manage the entire process.

The key is, if we're not monitoring the data and the way we do business, then there's no need to agree on how we do business. When we monitor it, we hold one another accountable. If a glitch shows up in the manufacturing process, the billing process, whatever particular system it is, then we catch it at the end of the shift, during the shift or whenever the data is collected. It's very important that we monitor the procedures we have and hold one another accountable with data. When we deal with data, we're making the right decisions.

A good example of collecting and qualifying follows: Production was 30% off during a particular shift. Paperwork (data) was collected, but no one looked at it. Later, we started pointing fingers and getting upset even though we didn't have a basis for our accusations. We discovered that the shift before us was shut down and they didn't give us their work until we were half way through our shift. In fact, the data showed that we worked much harder in the short amount of time we had that day. In fact, we accomplished 70% production in half the usual time. Here, we are not dealing with data, certainly not qualifying

it. We need to review the data that has been collected by asking the proper questions, not unnecessarily pointing fingers or accusing someone unjustly. Formal systems to train and teach management should be installed. If we get those systems, it is then the employee's job to monitor and manage the systems.

If we have a system or procedure, it needs to be documented in written form. If it is in writing, then we can manage that information and data. If we're collecting and managing, then we need to monitor; if we're not monitoring, then we need to be asking if the data is worth collecting. A lot of work being done in a given day is not being monitored, much less managed, thus allowing many people to waste a great deal of time.

We were collecting a piece of complex paperwork in a company where the paperwork affected five BaseWork Centers. When we tried to find the ownership of it, we found that no one even needed the form. All the information was being covered with another piece of documentation. It was taking a lot of time, energy, effort and money to complete this paperwork and get it to the five BaseWork Centers. When we finally started working through the form's origin, it was discovered that it was started by a guy who had left the company 15 years earlier. The reason he initiated the form was because of a one-time problem. This duplication had been going on for 15 years. One manager admitted that every time they handled a piece of paper, it cost them 10 dollars. Qualifying and monitoring is not only an important logistical tool, but it is also a cost effective way of doing business.

> *#30* *To make decisions based on data, we must qualify the data, manage, and monitor the data. If we are not managing and monitoring the data collected, then we do not need to collect it.*

SUMMARY

In summary, the systems review is defined as looking at how business is conducted from the company's viewpoint. The way you do business and execute your day- to day running of the business is via systems. Systems are either implied or written.

Most of the time systems within a business structure just "happen" without guidelines. That is the manifestation of the hectic pace of running the company day to day. It evolves primarily from the one strong entrepreneur that built the business and who is the driving force behind it. The last thing a person thinks to do when working 16-hour days, is to define systems.

As sales increase at a tremendous pace and making money and cash flow become priority, people are hired to handle specific jobs. Somehow the written system(s) is put on the back shelf with the new employee(s). The only time a system is reviewed is when you are putting out a fire. The fires are left smoldering to reblaze at a later time.

Do you think your problem is unique? Don't be disappointed to discover that it exists in every organization to a greater or lesser degree. Who do you blame? The answer is no one. Why? Because the tool did not exist and no one seemed to have a solution. Now there is a solution, and that solution is BaseWork Systems 2000. It is the only tool that exists to integrate quality into every process that makes up the systems within an organization. Moreover, the BaseWork Systems 2000 has given management a system to direct, manage, and monitor the transition process. The company can now provide quality of systems and quality of life—both at work and home.

All employees will become focused on their job (BaseWork Center). Amazing things happen when an organization has all employees focused and moving in the same direction. Not only do the employees become more involved, but they are able to react to issues and resolve them quickly. The organization becomes pro-active rather than reactive. They are on a constant vigil for new opportunities both internally and externally.

System Flow Chart

Process 1	Process 2
From Bed to Work Process and Steps	**From Work to Bed Process and Steps**
1. Clock goes off	1. Punch out at work
2. Start coffee	2. Get into Car
3. Go to bathroom	3. Pull out of lot
4. Shower	4. Drive home
5. Clothes ready	5. Get out of car
6. Get dressed	6. Eat dinner
7. Eat breakfast	7. Get undressed
8. Read paper	8. Go to bathroom
9. Get into car	9. Set alarm clock
10. Drive to work	
11. Park in lot	
12. Get out of the car	
13. Punch in at work	

1. Beginning of the day I start my Process and Steps. From bed-to-work.
2. End of the day I start my Process and Steps. From work-to-bed.

IN REVIEW , YOUR PROCESS AND STEPS FLOW CHARTING

Process	=	Bed to work and back
Step	=	How to get from bed to work and back.
Procedure	=	The procedure for how you do each of the steps.
System	=	From bed-to-work, doing my job, returning home is my system from getting to work and back.

Note: The **Process** is your job, **Steps** are how you do your job and the **Procedures** get written from those steps.

WHAT'S NEXT

You're probably saying about now, "All this quality development talk is well and good, but how do I solve the myriad of problems that I encounter? I face all kinds of problems everyday; is there something in your quality program that can help?"

I'm glad you asked, because there most definitely is! Next, I want to explain several processes for handling problems. Since no company is without them, problems must be addressed as part of a good quality program.

10
FOUR PROBLEM-SOLVING PROCESSES

PROCESSES DEFINED

You know the funny thing about problems? They can be of an endless variety. Is there really a tried and true, proven, successful system for attacking all problems? I don't think so!

As I tackled the issue of solving problems, my ideal system became four different processes. I just couldn't find one system that could be used on all the problems we were encountering. The one system approach can have as many as fourteen steps, some of which are really complicated. They seemed to be designed for scientific problem-solving of a complex nature.

What I've found as I've been on-site under actual working conditions is that most problems are not complex. It has been my observation that when employees stayed within the rules and stayed in their area of expertise and control, most problems were fairly straight forward.

In fact, less than 2% of problems are complex. If they are complex, everyday employees won't be involved. The department manager or other specialists will be involved in the more complex issues. If the employees must be brought in, then I have developed a process to handle that.

Let's take a look at the four problem-solving processes:

> **PROCESS A—The Five Steps**
> **PROCESS B—The Task Team Format**
> **PROCESS C—The Directed Task Team**
> **PROCESS D—Quick Action**

PROCESS A—THE FIVE STEPS

Process A is used to solve 98% of the problems encountered and will be where most team members spend their time in solving the team's problems. I call this the **Five Steps** where employees are asking themselves the three W's: what, which and why, (Different from the usual W's, huh?)

Step 1.

Step 1 is **Brainstorming** for a problem. Employees ask themselves *what* are the problems in their BaseWork Center.

Step 2.

Step 2 is **Problem Selection**. Employees ask *which* problem the team will work on and write a problem statement.

Step 3.

Step 3 is the **Cause and Effect**. Employees ask themselves *why* the problem is happening. The team can usually come to a consensus agreement on the answer. Most of the time it was simply lack of written procedure.

One of the things they do before they move on, or before they start talking about the problem, is determine if there was a written procedure. If not, they have to define the procedure. The procedure defines the process or steps. Then if they can't agree on why it's happening or if it looks like there is more than one answer, they go to Step 4. Going to step 4 rarely happens.

Step 4.

Step 4 is called **Data Collection and Display**. Employees have to collect the data and display it to support the possible solutions to the problem. If employees have the data and it's outside their decision-making authority, then they have to present it for a buy-off from whoever can sign. Presentation for buy-off is step 5.

Step 5.

Step 5 is called **Presentation** as just discussed.

Most of the time the problem doesn't go further than the third step. Most of the problems have to do with simple issues; typically, they have to do with procedure. Remember the majority of the problems are due to the four barriers to quality. So, if employees agree, they do what is called spin-out. Spin-out occurs when the team reaches a consensus agreement on the solution.

SITTING ON THE SIDELINES

Story #31

As we start making decisions within an organization, we find some people just sitting on the sidelines. When we start to formalize the way we do business through development of processes and systems, someone has to make a decision on that particular procedure or BaseWork Center. That brings me to the next point. While trying to move the organization to make decisions, we always have people offering advice, but they don't step up to take ownership or get involved. They might point fingers and tell you yes or no, but they don't take responsibility. We must be conscious of those people sitting on the sidelines because they will be the first to criticize what we're trying to do. They always have the greatest advice and answers but don't want to get involved and take ownership of their decisions.

In negotiations, when someone puts an idea on the table, one of the easiest things to do is take that idea and pick it apart. Instead, we ought to be looking at what we can do to support the idea. The guy sitting on the sidelines offers all kinds of information but never a solution or a decision to get the group to the next step. If someone is willing to take ownership of a procedure or idea, chances are it will fly. Be aware of those sitting on the sidelines, because the company will end up spinning its wheels and never make decisions.

> #31 *Sitting on the sidelines is comfortable if you are a spectator; however, building a quality company is not a spectator sport.*

PROCESS B—The Task Team Format

Process B is the **Task Team Format** which deals with how to write and implement a procedure. Anyone in the company can form a Task Team on any particular issue that is a problem. (Remember the welder from Chapter 8?) Typically, an employee has a problem that is getting under his skin and making life at work pretty miserable. This format is a vehicle for resolution of that problem.

The Task Team Format takes care of a lot of different things within the organization. The intent of the Task Team Format is to formalize how you write a procedure and the things that you do in order to make sure that the procedure is trained, logged, and implemented. It really becomes a formalized system. It is an extension of the problem-solving process. A lot of quality programs talk about task teams but one of the things that didn't exist was a process formalized to handle a task team.

SPONSORING OF A TASK TEAM

A Task Team can be comprised of workers from different jobs, departments, BaseWork Centers, and divisions. The Task Team is a way for anyone in the organization to address problems internally within the organization. Anyone in the company can sponsor a task team if they feel they have a problem.

To form a Task Team, an employee gets a Task Team Number from the coordinator of the quality program. Then the coordinator can log and manage the Task Team. One of the things the employee will do is project a finish date with time-tables. For example, the program coordinator makes sure whoever is sponsoring the task team lets their facilitator or boss knows that the task team has started. That is in the spirit of open and honest communication. Everyone should be working and informed. Communication is very important.

The sponsor of the Task Team is the person who is bringing up the issue or sponsoring that team. She needs to log her number, indicate where she's from and her BaseWork Center. Then she writes out a problem statement or selected problem. Also, she suggests a possible solution. She also states what she hopes to get out of it. Chances are the end result is going to be a written procedure for the problem statement. What you don't want is one person to run through the company sponsoring Task Teams that they have nothing to do with. The person sponsoring has to be involved in that Task Team.

The BaseWork Centers affected by the particular problem need to be addressed. You need to name one person to the team from each BaseWork Center affected. What that does is start to develop your team members for the Task Team. Also, you may need them as a resource. Once you gather the team together, make sure everyone understands and reviews the task and/or solution for clarity. Schedule your first meeting and then another meeting a couple weeks before your projected finish date. Be sure to schedule the meetings far enough in advance so team members can avoid scheduling conflicts and can attend the meetings.

The meetings will more than likely result in a new procedure. Complete a procedure form that properly identifies and assigns the procedure to the proper BaseWork Center. Log, manage, and monitor the action items and hold everyone accountable for them. Then, one of the most important things to do is complete the training and implementation form to make sure the solution or procedure is implemented. You can't hold anyone accountable until everyone has signed off on the training. Also, you need to determine whether a need exists to trial test or measure the solution. If the answer is yes, then collect data and make sure the decision made was the correct one. You will find that team consensus and agreement take a lot of effort and preparation. Determine if you must present it for approval. If yes, then you go to the Presentation Format.

TRAINING SOLUTION

When you complete the Task Team Form, determine who will do the training, the date, and the time of the training, and what BaseWork Centers need to receive the training. Consider what they'll use to train. Usually they'll use a written procedure that is on the flip chart. Make sure you have your agenda completed and on the flip chart for the training. Add the procedure to all the BaseWork Centers after the training and post the procedure on your E.I. (Employee Involvement) Board for all the team members to read.

Have all training materials approved by the coordinator. He is the one who will have to quarterback the whole program.

SUMMARY

In summary, the Task Team Format is a formalized way of organizing teams to address particular problems within an organization. The rules of the Task Team are that anyone in the company can sponsor a Task Team. It is a good formal process that can be managed and monitored regarding whatever particular problem you have. It doesn't matter whether it's from one BaseWork Center to another or one department to the next, or even from one division to the next. The key is that all employees within the organization receive training on the Task Team Format so when they sit down at a particular meeting, they understand the process. They understand what, where, and how they got there. They also need to understand the terminology. That's the great thing about having a Base Training Program for an entire organization. Everybody is on the same page, going in the same direction.

RICKY

Story #32

Ricky is an employee that worked his way up through the organization to a very important BaseWork Center in the accounting department. The program helped give Ricky a voice and input, not only in his job but in the program and its philosophy.

As Ricky grew and developed in the organization, he cultivated good friends who supported and believed in him. At the same time, he also had those that resented his accomplishments, discounted his wins and made excuses for his success. Ricky wasn't in the "clique" and was left out of many of the things that were going on.

As the program developed and we were brainstorming for problems, Ricky brought to light some major issues involving an important procedure in his department. As he pushed the issue and accountability for it, there was some resentment from his supervisors. They felt he was telling them what to do. As we worked through this in the program, we discovered that some of the people bringing conflict had been dodging responsibility.

With the program you can hide, weave, and manipulate, but you can only do so for so long. As the funnel concept works its way down, everyone will eventually be held accountable, not necessarily by management, but from one department to another. Ricky was able to address some things that were affecting his job in a negative fashion. He was not getting back information he needed to do his job correctly, and some of the information was from his supervisors.

Because of his positive level of involvement, management was able to see the real talent and skills possessed by Ricky. Even though they had previously recognized it with job promotions, they were now able to see hidden gifts and the talent Ricky brought to their organization. He is a first-class example of an employee who, when given an opportunity to do right and help the company, will step forth and do whatever he can to help the company.

> #32 *Some of the brightest talent in your organization have not yet turned on their lights.*

PROCESS C—THE DIRECTED TASK TEAM

Process C is **Directed Task Team**. This procedure is used in less than 2% of a company's problems.

Step 1.

Step 1 is usually sponsored by Leadership. The sponsor selects an issue or concern, typically of a somewhat complex nature and writes a problem statement.

Step 2.

Step 2 is choosing the team, which is usually done by the sponsor.

Step 3.

Step 3 concerns why the problem is happening since it has already been defined. The Directed Task Team has come to the decision that they've got a problem and they want to address it. Step 3 is the *Cause and Effect* investigating why it's happening. It can possibly spin out again, and go to the Task Team Format (B). If they can't spin it out they may have to go to Step 4.

Step 4.

Step 4 is data collection and display.

Step 5.

Step 5 is implementation and or training.

Step 6.

Step 6 is presentation.

Step 7.

Step 7 is trial test and/or tracking.

PROCESS D—QUICK ACTION

Process D is a **Quick Action**. Quick Action is defined as items that are *small* problems (no more than two are addressed at one time) in the work group's area of responsibility (BaseWork Center) and hands-on expertise. The problems have an obvious, quick consensus solution that can be authorized by the leader/facilitator and implemented by a member or the leader in one to four hours of individual effort over a one- to four-week period of time. The team has to reach a consensus that it is a quick action.

I have found very few problems that cannot be solved using one of the four processes. Even though they may appear somewhat involved on paper, actual workplace implementation is a snap. The secret is that they allow employees to solve their own problems in an open and honest fashion without a lot of negative finger pointing. All energy is channeled in a positive fashion toward problem solution as opposed to problem blame.

JUSTIFY AND DEFEND

Story #33

There is a cardinal rule when addressing conflict related to a quality issue. Resolve the issue without getting personally involved. Don't try to pin the blame. The objective is to resolve the issue—not find a scapegoat.

In addressing conflict, sometimes we feel someone has to leave the meeting with the blame. There is a problem with that approach. Even if you have tons of evidence on a person proving him wrong, the person will justify and defend every action he has taken. Whether he is right or wrong, has hidden agendas or not, he believes what he did was right and he has a rational reason to justify and defend it. Everyone then gets defensive and tries to justify. The ensuing debate ends up having nothing to do with what you were talking about.

Let's step back and cool off a bit. Our intent is to solve the issue, not to pin blame. When you seek to solve, you move through the issue and come to an agreement for solution.

Remember, the old school is to pin the blame. Once people feel they are held accountable, they'll think twice before they do something wrong because of the accountability. We need to take responsibility for these people. Because of the lack of systems and accountability within an organization, the company must accept the responsibility. If he is, in fact, a bad employee, then that will surface and come to light. He will force himself out of the program. He can no longer hide and the funnel concept will click into action.

> #33 *When addressing employee conflict, remove your and the company's emotions from the deal and deal only with facts and data.*

PART III

Okay, by now you probably have a pretty good understanding of the problems and the solutions. After a company has BaseWork Systems 2000, fear has been removed, the lines of communication opened, procedures have been written and employees trained and skilled. The organization is now a formal organization. The company's other issues can now be solved by task teams developed within the organization. The company is now in the position where continuous progress and improvement are assured.

You may now be asking yourself why you should use my program instead of one of the others on the market. After all, I haven't discussed buzz words like "continuous improvement" or "statistical process control" in any great detail. In part III, I intend to cover these two buzz words (phrases) in particular. See if you agree with my thinking.

Part III is the fun part. It contains true stories that happened during the nine years BaseWork Systems 2000 program was created. If you look hard, you can see yourself in the stories.

11

CONTINUOUS IMPROVEMENT

The average employee wandering around your company hallways and production aisles doesn't really have a clue about the real meaning of *continuous improvement*. Your employees are smart people, so what is the problem? The problem is that the interpretation out in the business world by corporate executives and high dollar consultants doesn't make sense to day-to-day, hard-working, floor-savvy employees. First of all, the definition currently in vogue is way too complex for the average employee to understand. Continuous improvement has a thousand different definitions depending on to whom you're talking.

Current thinking (which is quite flawed in my opinion) causes companies to jump on a fast moving, problem-solving process or to blindly choose a quality program from the marketplace. They rush to brainstorm for problems, and are eager to improve while throwing in a little statistical process control for good measure.

THE PROGRAM OF THE MONTH

Story #34

Most organizations that are going through education and training of their employees are using a program that was reinvented from something they previously used; it's simply packaged a little differently.

Every other month there's a new buzz word. Although companies are searching for tools to make a difference in their organizations, consultants aren't really listening. They fail to consider the needs. They just continue to give them a rework of an old program.

You find that even though companies are buying the programs, they are spinning their wheels because the reworked program is taking them in no particular direction. They aren't talking and communicating with one another.

They may be fired up for a month or so on a new program and then the next month, it's something else. They aren't following through with anything. Soon the employees are desensitized and unaffected because it's just the program of the month. How long will this one last, a week, a month? How long will we stay excited about this, three days?

I believe the industry has done a poor job in meeting the needs of the market and is not listening to the needs of their customers. That's why I believe my program is unique. It was developed by our customers, on site, by the employees, under actual working conditions for 20,000 hours over seven years across several industries. Since it was developed by the people using it—it was tailor-made to meet their needs. That's why my program is so successful.

If we are not consistent with what we offer our customer, then we cannot expect to promote trust. Employees may spend a great deal of time and effort on a program only to find that in a relatively short period of time it dissolves and nothing comes of it. They develop an attitude that it's the last time they'll get involved because it was a waste of time. Remember, consistency promotes trust. Consistency proves to the employee that the company has a direction and purpose and the employee's best interest at heart. It promotes security.

When you step out and look at most of the programs available, they have absolutely no accountability and no monitoring, very little direction, and no documentation. They don't know where they'll end up, or even what they're going to do. Be aware of the consultant hook. Once they get in with an entry-fee product, they all of a sudden become a permanent staff member, constantly selling, always finding something new to introduce.

#34 *Beware of a new name for an old problem.*

My point is that you can't do any continuous improvement without first formalizing the way you're doing business. You have to build the business infrastructure!

In order to improve a system, you have to define the system. I've said this time and time again. When defining the system, you start flushing out problems and identifying solutions. In BaseWork Systems 2000, you develop a flowchart, define the systems, define the process, list the steps, and come to an agreement on the procedures. Implementation follows. Once you have a system in a controlled state, meaning it is pretty much running right all the time, then it's consistent and continually improving.

Continuous improvement should be simply defined as continually improving the way you do business. You can't do that until you have all the systems defined and every employee in the organization trained. Your employees must have the power to improve their processes, steps, and procedures, which in turn improves their BaseWork Center.

Such a dynamic process continually breathes new, innovative life into the system and company. Continuous improvement can't be a slogan; it can't be just employees or one department; it has to be everybody in the organization. Continuous improvement is not hard to accomplish if you dissect processes and the organization, BaseWork Center by BaseWork Center.

TOTAL QUALITY MANAGEMENT

Story #35

TQM (Total Quality Management) has been a buzz word for ten years. The concept encapsulates Dr. Deming's philosophy.

TQM has gotten a lot of bad rap. Many consultants have gone into companies with different interpretations of what TQM means. Everyone has their own ideas and beliefs of what quality is.

The problem with the TQM philosophy in business today is that companies treat it like a cafeteria. They pick and choose what they want to take out of total quality management and leave the rest of the program.

For example, managers don't necessarily want to look at documenting the systems, but they want to cut costs. Their solution is to cut payroll. That's TQM? They take the simple things that fit or the easiest things for them to handle and implement little pieces of them.

TQM will not work without total commitment. You can't steal second base and keep your foot on first. You hear a lot about re-engineering. Companies are out-sourcing and down-sizing themselves to death. Those strategies just don't work.

Buzz words used by most consultants don't have much depth to them or foresight, because the consultants have never really been in the workplace to see if they work.

With TQM or BaseWork Systems 2000, our philosophy is that you can't have total quality management without having every process, step, procedure, system, department, and division in the organization going in the same direction and being held accountable. There is absolutely no other way. I feel that has failed in the marketplace. There has been no tool to implement quality in every process within that organization. There has been no way to hold everybody accountable for **breaking through the four barriers to quality**.

TQM has gotten a bad rap. A lot of people simply don't understand it. They digest what they can but only get a little good out of it. Most people have no concept of what a commitment TQM takes to make it work. You cannot be half committed.

> #35 *Total Quality Management must be placed in the hands of the employees with leadership from a totally committed management.*

STATISTICAL PROCESS CONTROL (SPC)

Let's take a moment to examine one of the popular buzz words you hear so much about: Statistical Process Control (SPC). SPC can be based on formulae requiring data collection from complex processes, or it can be

some guy keeping a tally on a sheet of paper taped to the wall. The bottom line is that SPC tries to compute quality mathematically.

If you are an SPC officiator, please remember the need for historical perspective. You cannot just collect current data, but you need back data as an indicator of quality trends in your company.

As you look at SPC, you're looking at how you're doing business and how the particular system or process is running based on collectible data. That's all you're doing. You make decisions based on data that tell you what you can or can't do, how or when, and if it's acceptable or not acceptable. Statistical Process Control doesn't have to be a complex thing.

You use the same terminology, numbers, and information for the things you do day in and day out. There is no need to create complex formulae or flowcharts, implement complicated software programs, or any other such thing. All you need to do is break data down by BaseWork Centers. You statistically process and control. You collect data on what you're doing and get real averages. You get upper and lower ranges and find out what is acceptable or not acceptable

The customer will tell you what is or isn't acceptable; that will give you data. Economics typically drive customers' specs or the company's concerns (usually to make money). Is it a reasonable return? Are you producing it so you can make a profit? To collect usable data for SPC purposes, define how you're doing business, get everyone involved and deal with real numbers.

SUMMARY

The company must monitor data, information, processes, and systems. If you're collecting data and not using it for decisions, you might as well not collect it. If, however, you are going to collect data, it must be collected by managers and employees in every department with an eye toward monitoring BaseWork Centers.

That is all continuous improvement is—collect data and figure out if you can make money or not. Is it what the customer can use? Is it within their specs or the industry's specs? There will be parameters, but quality is not difficult. The easiest way to ensure its presence, is to get everyone involved. Remember, continuous improvement is not an option; it is mandatory for every employee in every organization.

TOO COMPLEX

Story #36

Most existing programs, training, and tools that the CEO and management have sound good and are packaged nicely. The terminology is "state of the art." They use all the current and common buzz words and sound beautiful. They're presented well by a professional salesman because they are very complex. Let's not talk about the fact that she may never have been into or made any changes in a company. Most quality and training programs out there are way too complex. We make business, then, too complex.

I have seen, for example, in accounting, countless ratios and numbers we can pull. Do we really need that many ratios to effectively run our organization? What we end up doing is spending a great deal of time creating all these fancy reports that no one probably ever sees, reviews, or even understands.

Instead, just figure out what we really need to run our business. What is it we need to communicate down through the organization? What will help our employees run our business and become more effective?

For example, we get a computer software program that has many uses. Why did we really get this program? All we want to do is manage our business. All our employees really want, when given this new computer program, is a good, simple tool to help them complete their job. They don't need to telecommunicate with masses of companies in multiple data banks. All they need is information and training to help them do their job competently and to the best of their ability.

With a new computer system, we may only need five functions but are given 2,000 and trained on 200. Everything becomes too cloudy and too difficult for the employees to digest.

Most companies don't have formal training programs and most existing products train off their technical manuals. They never think of processes, steps, and BaseWork Centers. Everything, then, gets very complex.

We also have fancy compensation programs. If you do x, y, and z, then you get this. Then we spend most of our time trying to figure out how that compensation or incentive plan is designed to motivate everyone to work harder and better and make more money. We should be asking, "why are we doing this"?

History has shown that if we put a system in place based on work quotas and performance goals, it can really turn around and become a negative. What if someone gets a bonus by selling eleven widgets this month, but I've only sold nine? I then give a large discount, promising unrealistic things and raise my sales to eleven. All of a sudden the increased need for product shows up in manufacturing. We now discover that we can't produce it fast enough.

The salesman gets his bonus, but the guy in manufacturing lost his because he can't meet the production level created by the salesman. We have to move away from this kind of incentive. The real incentive should be to improve the way we're doing business.

Let's find those tools for training and for developing systems and processes. Let's look at how we can basically do business better.

The bottom line is, we want to make more money and we think we can motivate our employees by paying them more. Compensation does not make a difference if we don't have the systems and processes in place and if we're not monitoring them. You can pay employees 50 dollars an hour, but in the long term, it won't make a difference. Show me a long-term incentive program that works. I haven't seen it.

This once again brings up the double standard. Why should the guy in sales get paid a double commission for selling x, when the people that process the paperwork, or the person inventorying isn't getting anything. We start making things so complex, when all we really need to do is improve business. The program's position is that management has not had a tool to make the difference or change.

We are bombarded with big lawsuits and publication notices of all these companies being sued because of safety.

We've got a new safety law to make sure all companies have a safety program. Well, if you read through HazMat law, it's so difficult to understand, complex, and frustrating that most companies don't have enough money to implement the thing. To make it work, they need to hire a human resource person, a consultant, or an attorney for HazMat.

What we really need to do is look at the intent of the laws. It is to provide safety for our employees. We have to put into place the systems, processes, and procedures to make this happen.

If you look at the major lawsuits, they result because a problem was brought up and management didn't have the systems, processes, or the accountability to address the issue. Even though it was documented, it was never taken care of. The lawsuit came about because the company was negligent with a hazardous issue and didn't address or resolve it. Again, the systems and processes are not in place. There is not a company out there that will get sued for trying to do the right thing and diligently working to have the vehicles in place. Deliberate malice and neglect are what cause lawsuits.

Another thing that can be too complex within an organization is the phone system. We may only need a few simple functions such as accepting the call, putting them on hold, transferring calls, and a voice mail system. Instead we have a complicated system that we need to read a manual to understand. It takes thirty steps to program and recall it. The manual doesn't get read. Money is wasted because of these unused functions.

If you look, that's what has happened with all the technology and information. We keep adding and adding instead of sifting through it— determining what we don't need. The salesman can make something sound and look great, but how do you use it in the workplace? Things are too complicated because many times the employees using the system are not involved in the decision to upgrade.

This country spends two-thirds of its time marketing a product and only one-third of the time on the process, whereas in Japan, it is the opposite. They spend two-thirds of their time developing the process and one-third of the time on sales. My parents bought a new faucet from one of the number one faucet companies in the nation. They have an 800 number for service. It sounded great but it took them two weeks to get through. The company marketed the product well, but had only one 800 number and one operator to handle all the calls for service. They never anticipated this was going to happen when they offered this service. Why? Because they hadn't done their homework on the process.

Most of the things that have happened involving the complexity of the office have happened because we've allowed them to happen. We've allowed complex technology to take over. Let's back off and get the employees involved. Let them help us find out exactly what we do need, so that when we do buy it, it is because of their direction and input.

> #36 *Taking one step away from logical thinking and common sense, is a step in the wrong direction.*

A Positive Note

A company can take on building business infrastructure—when the employee doing the job defines their "BaseWork Centers", process, steps and procedures.

With employee involvement the transformation from an informal to a formal organization can take place during regular business hours without shutting down the day-to-day running of the business. "Your employees can figure it out"—just give them the responsibility and the leadership.

Bruce

WHAT'S NEXT

You can stop reading now, if you want to do so! I think I've explained my system in enough detail that you have a basic understanding of how it works. If I've captured your interest, however, keep reading.

Next, I have added two chapters on additional stories and "Life's Lessons" respectively. I think you'll enjoy reading them!

Chapter 12 specifically is a collection of additional stories plus an interview, none of which were used elsewhere in the book. Each, in its own way, goes a little further in reinforcing and/or introducing concepts central to my philosophy of quality. Even though this chapter is not critical to your understanding of the book, I recommend reading it. You might just learn something!

Bruce

12
MORE STORIES

SMALL BUSINESS

Story #37

Small businesses usually begin when an employee working for a larger company leaves and starts a similar business. The person in this story started out in sales. While working for his original company, this person made the sale, delivered the product, collected the payment, and processed the paperwork. Additionally, he had to fight the battles with manufacturing regarding marketing and other product issues.

Since he felt he was performing all aspects of the business, he decided to do it for himself. The entrepreneur wants to control his destiny; he is tired of working for other people. The main reason for this is that there is so much internal chaos in the average company.

The first thing the small businessman does when starting a business is design some type of management structure. Ideally, he wants some type of training and good solid management systems. This new business owner plans to listen to his customers and treat his employees fairly.

Since this entrepreneur is cash stricken from the beginning, his highest priority is to go out and start generating sales as quickly as possible. In the beginning, he finds himself doing everything. As sales get larger, he begins hiring a person here and there.

As the business grows, the owner begins to fumble the ball. He personally tries to explain the paperwork and business processes to the employees. Even though he has noble intentions of thoroughly training his employees, it does not happen—time is working against him.

In many of these small businesses, sales take off and the company grows rapidly. In no time, the entrepreneur loses track of what is going on internally. He starts seeing problems here, there and everywhere. Much to his surprise, the problems are the same as those left behind at the old company. The entrepreneur has become what he hated; he has become the old company.

One example of this is a group of individuals that left a rather large company and started their own company. They vowed that one of the things they would do was train and be the best in the industry. As they grew, they fell into the same old loop as everybody else. They had 30, then 100, then 300 employees—yet conducted no formalized training. Soon, they found themselves losing control. Just like the entrepreneur above, the new company had become the company they wanted to leave behind.

Another example was a group of people that had left a company to start a similar business. They took a lot of key personnel with them from the company they left behind. The man for whom they had worked was not an easy going guy. In fact, he abused his employees and they literally hated him.

The man had made a lot of money with skyrocketing sales in spite of his abusive personality. As a result, the group left. They wanted to *do it right* and have the employees become truly a part of the company. They wanted a change in philosophy that would ensure that they would never become what they had left behind. Their plan was to structure the company with solid participatory management procedures. You can guess what happened! Before management strategies could be implemented, they started having problems. All of a sudden, the entrepreneurs were doing the ole' management two-step. Putting out fires became the order of the day. The participatory management procedures never got defined and the training never got structured. The CEO, however, was bragging about what a great company he had—and according to him, everything was fine. No one could talk to the CEO for fear of losing his/her job or having the CEO get mad.

The man telling me this story told me that the situation they were in was exactly what they had left behind in the old abusive company. As you remember, they swore that would never happen, but it did.

Most small companies don't plan on being big companies; it just kind of happens. Most big companies with whom I have worked started out small. That probably explains why they never seemed to develop their business properly. Most are really inadequate in relation to process and steps. That's why I feel our BaseWork concepts and structuring of organizations are so important for the continuing success of businesses.

> #37 *The best time to build business infrastructure is at the business conception and start. The best time is before you don't have time.*

QUALITY ISSUES

Story #38

As the program progressed, there was a need starting to develop for policies regarding the interaction between management and employees. The rules of my program are that if we are to communicate, we must do so in writing.   We find the policies and procedures are at times not being monitored, followed, or enforced. We have employees that continued to have conflict with their supervisors and feel powerless to make changes. They point fingers at the program and say they were told the company was going to do what was morally and ethically correct, and to treat everybody as they wanted to be treated.   The supervisors, however, were not acting on the quality issues in this fashion.

One of the employees in particular was very pro-active with the program, had gotten very active in the teams, and was very outspoken. If the company is not acting in a morally and ethically correct fashion, then this type of employee can be earmarked by management as a trouble-maker and targeted for either disciplinary action or termination. To prevent this, the employees must be protected through procedures built into the system.

This employee came to a meeting one day and on his way out the door, his supervisor jumped on him, saying that the only reason he wanted to be in the meeting and participate was because he was lazy and didn't want to do the work.

I had just finished the meeting and was doing some paperwork. The employee approached me and told me his boss had just come out and read him the riot act and accused him of being a poor, lazy employee. He said to me, "That isn't quality."

I had to agree with him. My dilemma was that they had the policies and procedures to protect employees, but they weren't being enforced. It's really a sticky situation when you go into a company and are ensured of fair treatment for participating employees, only to observe the opposite. Even though protection procedures were in place, no one was monitoring or enforcing what was happening.

This was when I had to decide how we would develop what we now call Quality Issues. How are we going to write up a procedure for what happens in a conflict between employees and management or a conflict with someone not doing his job? How do we write policies and procedures for all this without having a manual 400 pages thick?

Two rules that I had been taught by my parents and grandparents, things that we lived by, were that you do things that are morally and ethically correct and you treat everybody as you want to be treated. These are a bit vague but are basically fundamental rules to live by. When in conflict with one of these, it becomes a quality issue.

The coordinator of the quality program must address the quality issues. We asked the CEO to sign off and commit to it; we wrote it up and posted it; and it became a part of the class training. We began talking about quality issues.

One of the employees came up with a quality issue and I approached management with it. Management started attacking me saying I didn't have my information correct. This was hearsay and the employees told me what they want me to hear because I had no idea what really happened. They wanted to know who said it and I told them I wouldn't tell them because of the fear of repercussions.

Management then turned a deaf ear saying there was nothing to what I had told them. My job then was to figure out the best way to approach this issue. I went to the employee and suggested we write it up. The employee was afraid he would be fired or his boss would know who it came from and would make his life so miserable he would be forced to quit. I realized this was a real problem because many of the employees felt the same way.

I then developed a quality issue form. This form had some basic statements such as, what is the issue, what would you recommend as a solution, and who are the people involved. The employee also had the option to sign it.

Our position was that if it was a problem, we must try to correct it. We don't defend whether it is right or wrong, or justify the problem. If that employee feels it is a problem, then it must be addressed.

Most of the time management will say, "It's not a problem, he just thinks it's a problem." An outgrowth of this was the development of a format on how to address quality issues. We did not pin blame on any one person; we tried to get both sides to look at the issue and see there was a problem and seek to resolve it. We don't care who did it— that is not our objective. In most instances, conflict resolution is a complex issue and someone feels he has to win. My program states that 99% of the people within a given organization are good and want to do what is right.

We take the position that there is lack of communication or understanding of another person's needs. We need to get them to state their position, think about it, and then walk out of the room and still say hello to each other.

Many of the quality issues have to do with management conflict at first. They may not have started out to be major issues, but the employee will build it up to one because it will fester and no one would address it and it keeps getting worse. Everyone begins complaining.

So, as the quality issue developed, we allowed the employee to write up the form with the option to sign it and then deal with the issue. We make sure everybody understands that it will not become a part of the personnel package of the individual.

We are not defending whether the issue is right or wrong; someone merely feels they have a problem. We have to be conscious of the concern of this employee.

Management was afraid of the employee with regard to conflict. Once management saw that no one was going to come down on them, everyone began to relax and we were able to talk about these issues.

Soon, it spread throughout the company that we were, in fact, addressing issues. Sometimes, for the first time in the company's history, we are able to address conflict between employees and management. This is a boost to morale, helps lower defenses, and starts promoting trust on both sides—for management and employee.

With the success of Quality Issues, I decided to offer a workshop detailing its development and use. Quality Issues don't just have to be conflict in regard to employees or management; it also has to do with some of the policies the company has. It has to do with the way business is done within the company.

The employee can write a quality issue, for example, on the paperwork he might be using that he feels is incorrect. He can write it up on what he thinks it should be. Later on, we will discuss how employees learn to address these as Task Teams.

> #38 *You can't have quality before you have a base foundation of doing what is morally and ethically correct, treating everybody as you want to be treated, and holding everybody accountable for that treatment.*

PROCESS D—QUICK ACTION

Story #39

Quick action is Process D of the Four Problem-Solving Processes. I developed quick action because we saw that a lot of the problems within our companies were not complex problems.

Some of the rules for quick action are: it must be obvious to the team; the team must reach a consensus on the solution; and the solution must be documented.

When we are in a meeting, we may begin with the lights off. We ask the question, "Why are the lights off?" We go to the switch and turn the light on. It was obvious why the lights were off and the solution was simple. That is what we mean by quick action. It must be obvious to the team and they must come to a consensus or agreement.

One of the problems in training is that the employees want to look at everything as a quick action. For example, overtime is up, so stop overtime. That's a quick action.

My position is that we need to be asking why is the overtime happening and is it in anybody's particular job function, route, service, product, or shift. Most managers just put our fires. They deem that as a quick action. Maybe management is told to cut it's cost 10% in his process, system, or shift. It then lays off one person. To management she has resolved the issue of the 10% cost reduction in her department.

But what we need to do is ask why our cost is up 10%. How can we improve the way we are doing business internally so that we can improve our process or system?

Again, one of the things companies do is just cut expenses. I agree that needs to be done. But there has to be a reason behind it. We may cut payroll, but we need to look at how we are doing business—the process and system—and make it more cost-effective.

Everyone may cut expenses 10% but in a different way. Our job is to show and direct management how to do that. Most of management put out small problems by temporarily resolving them; then they go on to the next problem without having really fixed the first one. It's a continuous loop. Each fire is left smoldering and will start up another day unless you improve the system, define the problem and put a permanent solution into place.

> #39 *We must move the quick fix, quick action, putting out the fire, instant gratification mentality to a long-term process of system improvement. Instead of jumping to the quick fix or quick solution, we need to ask why is that problem happening.*

OPEN DOOR POLICY

Story #40

Do you know what is really strange? Most of our CEO's and presidents of companies really believe that they have an open door policy. What happens as a company grows, especially from starting up as a mom-and-pop family-owned business, is that they do have an open door policy in the beginning. They are interacting daily, even hourly, with their employees.

Early on, the CEO of the company remembers what it was like when he worked for somebody else. So, he has the best intentions of keeping an open door policy stating that, if they have a problem, the employees should come to him.

His commitment and desire is to allow the employees to express their concerns. He wants to be there for them and help rectify any problems that arise.

As the company grows, departmental walls form and the company loses that CEO/President personality. The president no longer hires people and no longer communicates with everybody, because he now has many other responsibilities.

The new standing rule in the business is that you must work through the chain of command. CEO's respect their management and try to work within the formal structure.

Because many managers haven't developed skills or haven't been trained in the position, they don't really understand what the job entails. So, when someone approaches them with a problem or concern or even a good idea for solving that problem, they are intimidated. A lot of them take it personally and conclude that they aren't doing their job correctly. They don't understand that their job should be to encourage. Because they don't really understand their job, they don't know what they're supposed to do.

The CEO truly believes he has an open door policy. But if someone is seen walking across the parking lot to his office, or makes an appointment to have coffee with him, everyone jumps to conclusions immediately and starts thinking the worst. Usually there is good reason for these conclusions, because most managers, at one time or another, have had a bad experience with someone trying to go behind their back with a hidden agenda.

The employee may have success reaching the CEO, but it will eventually filter down to him that if he tries it again, he could very well lose his job or, at the least, end up with some kind of a penalty—maybe working the graveyard shift. Managers won't come right out and say it, but it is directly or indirectly applied through other employees or other management. That employee then becomes a shut-down employee.

This is why we talk about fear and this is why there is no open and honest communication until we remove the fear. If the CEO were to find out, he would get upset and wonder why no one told him about this incident. Ultimately, the element of fear paralyzes all communication to some degree or other.

So, for us to assume that most companies have an open door policy is not correct. When we say there should be a free flow of information, we mean that information goes both ways. Anyone should be able to talk to anybody within a company, including the CEO, and ask an open and honest question and get an honest answer without fear of reprisal. Perhaps the CEO may complain that everyone is wanting to come up and talk with him; but isn't that what you want within your company?

| #40 *The open door policy in most organizations is shut.* |

GENE

Story #41

Gene is a perfect example of what my program brings out in an employee. He was with one of our companies and was the youngest employee in manufacturing. Gene had been with this company for a couple of years and had a great deal of enthusiasm.

When we begin my program, we are always looking for someone to take on the job as coordinator for BaseWork Systems 2000. Gene agreed to this responsibility. He is an exceptional young person and will one day, I believe, be running his own company.

Gene had already tried to do a lot of things in the company, but the lack of systems and directions ended up beating him down. He kept taking on more and more projects but became disillusioned.

Gene was thrilled when my program was implemented. When we sat down and shared with him, he was pleased the company was willing to make this commitment and give him a tool to help straighten things out. The older employees were more negative and felt nothing would change.

Within six months into the program, Gene not only educated himself, but he got involved as coordinator and in task teams and had really grasped the concept of my program well. Gene ended up running manufacturing.

Gene has been with the business now for about four years and is 26 years old. This program brought out his hidden talents and apparent enthusiasm. He is a perfect example. All he needed to excel was the right tool, some encouragement, and trust in his management. With these things in place, all kinds of great things are happening.

Even though he had leadership potential all along, he wasn't in the previous management structure. My system allowed Gene to step up and become a leader.

> #41 *The life of an organization is the development and training of its greatest assets—its employees.*

LARRY

Story #42

Larry was employed in one of our companies but had been transferred from another division. When he got into the plant, all I heard was a lot of negative things about him from management.

Oftentimes, this type of negative feedback is indicative of jealousy. What this signifies is that the person possibly has some great talent and potential to offer the company and the negative comments are a defense mechanism that select management uses to get rid of the competition.

Many of the people sending out negative rap on an individual have simply learned how to manipulate the information that is going to the CEO/President of the company. They know just what to say and how to say it, so when the CEO steps back from it, then it sounds logical and seems to have merit.

Larry had just been brought into this division when we started the program. We needed some help with our Spanish-speaking employees. We needed somebody out in the plant that could speak Spanish and English.

So, we asked Larry if he would get involved. He agreed and also translated our written English into Spanish. He did a beautiful job of it! You can take one paragraph of English and it translates to multiple paragraphs in Spanish. This is a unique talent that not too many manufacturing people have.

Larry translated my program and was a team leader of not just one but two teams. It was clear that the Spanish employees had a lot of respect for Larry.

As the quality program continued, Larry was getting constantly moved around by management. I expressed my concerns and supported Larry and asked them to allow him to devote more time to the program. Because even the CEO was impressed with Larry, he was given an opportunity to correct himself as the program developed.

Larry oversaw a department in the plant. I walked into the plant one day and he was using creative ideas with hoses and pipes and was experimenting within his job. He was keeping written data and information about those experiments.

About six months down the road some of management started complaining that my program wasn't working and they were tired of trying to make it work. But their CEO said it was already working because Larry had cut the cost of doing business in his particular department. That was proof the program worked.

Here was an employee that would probably have slipped through the cracks in this organization and his potential would not have been utilized had my program not given him an opportunity to step up and shine.

As the program continues within an organization, it becomes less dependent on management and the president of a company being involved and more dependent on program leaders, facilitators and coordinators like Larry. Titles within the company become less important. Larry is still making a difference in the company.

#42	*The most undervalued asset in an organization is its employees and their potential.*

YOU CAN'T IMPROVE ON THE OUTSIDE UNTIL YOU IMPROVE ON THE INSIDE

Story #43

After my initial work with the program, I became aware that you can train and do a lot of things for an organization, but if you are not training and educating the employees with basic interpersonal skills, whatever training you do will be short-lived.

A lot of us have negative baggage we carry with us. It may come from school, TV, print, or our environment. We can't help somebody improve on the job until they improve mentally and emotionally. To do this, we point at our head and at our heart.

We become aware of why certain things are happening. Some of us live from one crisis to the next. We all know somebody like this. They can't talk about anything unless it's a tragedy. Even when the current tragedy winds down, it is soon replaced by another tragedy.

Their whole lives are going in a negative sphere—from one negative to the next. These people never are happy. That negativity is all they have to hold on to, as ridiculous as that might seem. It may be the only thing in their life over which they feel they have control or of which they feel a part. Some of their friends and families have the same tendencies.

We make our employees aware by teaching them a simple philosophy called **SMILE. SMILE** is an acronym for *"a **S**mile in the **M**orning **I**mproves **L**ife **E**veryday."* We can either have a good day or a bad day. It is totally up to the individual. This way of thinking is simply to get everybody off to a good start in the morning.

This is an awareness of how we are doing things and how we are programmed to respond to one another. A lot of people are programmed for defeat or sadness. It's just as easy to program ourselves for happiness.

Mentally we need to be aware of why things are happening. In our hearts we want to be that good person. Many times this is taken from us in subtle ways during our lifetime. We see it all around us. The media is mostly negative, and then life, in general, becomes negative.

We need to change this at work and encourage employees to do what is morally and ethically correct and treat everybody as they would want to be treated.

Yes, we do have some people that resist, but I have found that these people have some real hidden problems. These people just can't see themselves as being happy.

In order for this to start taking place in their lives, my program sets the pace at work and starts asking questions about family, and asking if the employee is having a good day. There is no way you can separate your work life from your home life, or visa versa. If you have a bad day at work, when you walk in the door at home, it will be apparent to everybody.

Companies do themselves a big favor by equipping their employees with these positive emotional and mental tools. Once they start making these changes at work, it will be carried with them to their home lives. Work can't improve until the employee's outlook and attitude improves. We can go in with all kinds of training and great programs, but if you have that underlying negativity, nothing will change.

> #43 *An employee's quality of work is in direct correlation with their quality of mental and emotional well-being.*

IMPROVING THE PROCESS CUTS EXPENSES

Story #44

When most companies see their spending getting out of hand, their first thought is to cut line-item issues such as employees, service and expenses. My policy is that we can't simply cut costs; we must also improve the business.

We must ask why the expenses are out of line. Most operations managers are brought on to solve the problem. But what I see them doing is not improving operations, but often just acting like accountants who look at the statements and recommend maybe cutting 15% out of manufacturing or administration.

Our question to that is, "HOW do we cut that 15%?" We must improve our process, our systems and our business by 15%. The employees remaining after a budget cut may carry the company and do the additional work of their laid off colleagues, but after a while they become burned out and soon the decision-makers are saying, "We cut 15%, now let's cut 5% more."

We have to control our costs and the only way we can do that is to define how we are doing business. Line-item management in the long run is cutting your way right to disaster. If our expenses are out of line, we need to step back and ask why.

Just a note, if everything is operating at full efficiency then cutting 10%-15% could be a problem. Remember when making decisions, make them only with data and the workers should be included in those decisions. If we are not efficient, then this puts pressure on becoming more efficient.

There are some things that will need to be cut up front, but there must be a balance. It all must be planned, directed, managed, and monitored with everybody going in the same direction.

You see companies laying off 4,000 employees. My question is how did they get to that point where there was a need to lay off that many people? And secondly, the systems and processes haven't been defined, so how are they going to do that? Is there a plan? No. There is internal chaos without any long-term forethought as to where we will end up.

#44 *Line-item management hardly ever provides long-term solutions for the improvement of the way we are doing business.*

THE FUNNEL CONCEPT

Story #45

In all companies, we immediately see people point fingers at different departments, different profit centers, different jobs, different systems, and at different employees saying, "That is where the problem lies." Instead of acting with a knee-jerk reaction, my policy is that we all start on an even scale because we feel that 99% of our employees are good people. Incomplete or undefined systems and processes have made employees less than good performers. It is totally the companies' responsibility to take care of these inadequacies.

Many experts say that quality programs are an option. We disagree. In every company into which we go, there is no option. A quality program is a must. Everyone is asked to participate and no one is exempt. The people that do the most complaining about quality programs are those that have figured out how to beat the system in an environment that has no structure.

The funnel concept says we all start equally at ground zero. We don't push or demand. We funnel everything down. What we have found is that people will commit to the program at different times. There will be those unique individuals who jump on right at the beginning and volunteer to be a coordinator. Then you will have others waiting to see if their friends will buy into the program. Then there's another group that has a critical eye and wonders whether this is just the latest program of the quarter. They may have committed to a prior program and did some work and the program dissolved before the improvements could be implemented. So they start out with negative feelings about the program.

After 8 to 14 months in my program, the employees start seeing the consistency and commitment of management and this promotes trust. Everyone is held accountable, not just some of the time, but all the time. Leadership must lead the charge. The employee sees management addressing quality issues and sees that everybody is treated fairly and there are no personal attacks. The program simply attacks the issues.

We have found that statistically only 1% of the employees funnel out of the program. These employees were a problem before the program was implemented, and they now blame the program for everything. The areas with which they have the greatest complaints are absenteeism and tardiness to the program. This is because that 1% has never been held accountable and because there was a lack of accountability built into prior systems and processes in the company. The other employees begin holding them accountable. Good employees will not tolerate a double standard where somebody gets special privileges. That becomes a quality issue and we agree with them.

The more responsible employees have been upset with this 1% for years and will no longer tolerate their behavior. We see this very small percentage of employees being pushed down into the funnel, continuing to rebel and not handling the structure of the program and being held accountable. Eventually they funnel out and end up quitting.

My program is no more than 74 hours of training per employee. The reason it is a two-year process is because it takes time. Employees have to see a change of attitude and consistency that promotes trust. This takes place as we work on the four barriers to quality:

1. FEAR OF EXPRESSION OR ACTION
2. LACK OF VERBAL OR WRITTEN COMMUNICATION
3. LACK OF WRITTEN PROCEDURE
4. LACK OF TRAINING

Most programs don't work because the management and/or the employees don't give it enough time. They decide to move on, bringing in another concept and always ending up back at square one.

#45 *The program has found that 99% of employees in an organization are good employees. As the employees move through the program, we find that 5% of the employee base- resist the program for a variety of reasons. Statistically, 4% of that 5% get on board the program usually between months eighteen and twenty-four, leaving 1% of the employee base. Again, statistically, 1% of employees are bad employees, and they will remove themselves from the program, and more than likely from the company.*

NINETY-NINE PERCENT OF EMPLOYEES ARE GOOD PEOPLE

Story #46

Most people are very good people and good employees. We have found that 1% of the workforce and population are the reason we have laws and policies. This 1% learns to manipulate the lack of systems and procedures, not being held accountable, and lack of monitoring of the aforementioned. It adds up to lack of responsibility by that person and lack of accountability for his or her actions.

For example, in the workplace the bad employee has learned to manipulate the lack of systems and procedures and lack of monitoring within most companies. He has learned to manipulate other employees; he has learned to get his way; and he has learned to pass off his work onto others. He is usually the one that does most of the complaining, yet he'll never step up to bring a solution to the table.

As this continues, many of the employees that are around this person become disenchanted with the organization and the management. I have heard comments like,"I can't believe the company is letting this person do this."

What we find out is that the President certainly isn't aware of the problem and even his own manager is in the dark, sometimes. This is hard to believe for those in daily contact with him, but nobody knows how to handle it.

Most employees and managers avoid handling any kind of conflict because it is confrontational. Soon, a few years go by, and you see the good employees leaving, or transferring, because nobody wants to say anything bad about anybody.

The bad employee continues to bring havoc to the organization. The only way this person will settle down is to ensure that he is held accountable for his actions.

In my program, we find that 1%—the bad employees—seem to funnel out and leave. They hate the accountability and monitoring. Where we get them most of the time is with absenteeism and tardiness. They manipulate their managers, systems, and employees. They've always done what they wanted to do. They spend as much or sometimes more time trying to get around doing things than actually doing their work. It's something inside of them that can't really be explained. It seems logical to just get rid of them. But that rarely happens.

We end up making policies in most organizations out of a knee-jerk reaction to what this 1% has done and that frustrates the majority. For example: The coffee is missing. We know we didn't drink that much in a week. So the bad employee is stealing the coffee. The immediate reaction is no more coffee. But why should the 99% suffer and be insulted? Most people know who it is that's taking the coffee but nothing is done because there is not a system in place to hold the person accountable.

If you really look at the situation, this is a perfect example of the four barriers to quality: *FEAR*—fear of expression and/or actions; *COMMUNICATION*—verbal or written; *PROCEDURE*— most organizations have implied procedure, which allows this employee to manipulate it to fit his particular situation; and *TRAINING*—that's a cop-out for the 1% because they can use it as an excuse by saying that they didn't know any better. You can't manage or monitor it because it's not in writing. Because of these four barriers, that 1% has a haven for all his wrong-doings, whereas the other 99% are held hostage by the four barriers to quality and the lack of systems and by the 1% bad employees.

I've gone into companies and found this 1% and they have been there for a long time. Everyone knows who is a bad employee but no one is doing anything about it. No one is holding him accountable.

When the program is in place and everything is funneling down, we find we have nothing on the person in the files because nobody has monitored the procedures and held him accountable.

When the program is effective, many employees thought to be bad turn around and are positively influenced because most of them wanted to be a good employee and wanted to do what was right.

#46 *99% of the employees in an organization are good employees and accept and encourage accountability.*

THE ONE PERCENT

Story #47

What does this one percent look like? They usually have their own agenda. They are usually directly or indirectly an informal leader and they learn to manipulate other employees in what we call a negative rap. No matter what happens, there is always something bad going on or something bad that the company has done. By allowing this, the company permits this person to do what he wants to do. When you really look at them, they have a tremendous problem with absenteeism and tardiness both to the meetings and to work. The 1% move from crisis to crisis in their personal lives and in their business lives, and they walk around with a chip on their shoulder thinking the world owes them a living. Literally they believe that.

So this 1% of the employee base and population just create havoc on the entire organization. This person does not have a problem stretching the truth, or in fact, lying. He manipulates and doesn't care, because he doesn't feel responsible, because he's gotten away with it for so long. They can tear and rip a company apart while the other employees stand back—knowing the company must be aware. This misconception about company awareness ultimately causes hard feelings among the good employees.

Look at your own organization. We all know who that 1% are, but we have nothing in place to deal with them. We are told by attorneys and human resource professionals that we are powerless because there might be a lawsuit. That, in a sense, is holding the company hostage. But by not holding them accountable, they grow in strength and get other employees to shut down.

The worst thing we can do within a company is allow this 1% to run unchecked in the organization. We **must** hold them

196

accountable. This 1% is always talking bad about management, but when he talks directly to them, he acts like management's best friend. Management has learned to accept him as a great guy because he's telling management exactly what they want to hear. There are no consequences to telling or not telling the truth.

There is great conflict with the other 99% because they see what he gets away with and there truly is a double standard. If they did something wrong, then they would pay the consequences—but not the 1%. This is extremely frustrating. So how do we hold the 1% accountable? If we hold **everybody** accountable to the procedures and systems, you'll watch this guy squirm.

#47 *1% of the employees in an organization are bad employees that eat away at the integrity of an organization. Don't make rules directed at that 1% that affect the other 99% negatively, deal with the problem created by the 1%.*

PUT A NAME ON THE BLAME

Story #48

If you look at an organization with the intent to solve issues, problems, or concerns, most people will go into that situation with the idea that somebody has to lose. Someone has to be given the blame.

My program's position is that we don't care who is to blame. Our job is to fix the problem. When you try to pin blame on somebody, they will get defensive. The 1% are good at passing the blame, which infuriates everybody in the company.

My program doesn't care who it is or what it is; our job is to resolve the issue. We take our gloves off and work on the issue and not the personality or the person.

What we find is that the funnel concept comes into play and sooner or later the accountability takes care of the 1% that are causing the problems. We have to take the position that 99% of the employees are good people and want to do a good job. What we don't want to do is start attacking somebody for not doing their job. It is the company's responsibility when systems and processes are not in place. We should always assume that employees are trying to do their best.

Then we hear the 1% is doing one thing or another. They may get by with it one, two, even three times, but eventually, within the 24-month time period, that person will be held accountable or will leave.

Because of the issue of accountability, the "No Blame" concept, and dealing only with data, we feel my program can effectively take care of that small 1% that makes problems for the other

99% good employees. We don't need to allow that 1% to hold us hostage.

> #48 *When resolving issues, don't spend energy in a negative fashion by trying to justify or pin blame for that particular problem; spend that energy focusing on how to resolve the issue.*

A TOOL OF CHANGE FOR THE CEO

Story #49

If you really look at most organizations, the CEO is trying to do a good job. He usually is laboring under the old school of training that teaches the necessity for working within the parameters of the existing organizational structure.

If we are having a problem with a particular department, whether it be sales, production, service, manufacturing or warehousing, we have to work that particular problem through the respective manager or division vice president. Most CEO's try to respect that person and the normal chain of command. What we often find, however, is that the manager upon whom the CEO is relying has no real training in handling the conflicts.

So, the typical scenario has the CEO trying to hold things together by addressing a problem with the manager; the manager then goes to the employee and, via his attitude, shuts down the communication.

We all tend to point to the CEO as the person ultimately responsible for problems. Until BaseWork Systems 2000 was developed, there was no tool the CEO could use to take care of all the problems within the organization.

Take the four barriers to quality as an example. CEO's have human resource people trying their best to provide training and do what's right for the organization. But, inadvertently, barriers are being raised. When the CEO mandates cutting expenses, everyone applies their own interpretation of how to cut expenses and before you know it, they are just cutting line item-issues and never improving the way they are doing business. The next quarter those numbers look great and everyone has accomplished the required expense cuts. But what happens then? Those numbers will start showing up down the road in some other department or some other way.

The existing quality programs on the market don't reach every BaseWork Center in an organization. What we experience is erratic behavior with them going this way one quarter and another way another quarter. With my quality program, in 24 months the CEO will know every process and system and probably every employee in his organization, possibly for the first time. And also for the first time, he can hold everything, every process, and every person accountable.

My experience has convinced me that most CEO's are great people, but for far too long they have lacked a tool to make meaningful organizational change regarding their companies' culture, process, systems, and procedures.

> #49 *In order for an organization to become a quality organization, the owner/CEO/President has to have total support and buy off from his board as well as the shareholders. In doing this, he must move from short-term thinking to long-term planning and direction. The CEO must lead this transformation via available tools designed to manage and monitor the process through accurate data.*

STARS SHINE FROM WITHIN

Story #50

Most organizations have many employee *stars*. These stars are usually relatively new to the company. They have yet to be beaten down by the lack of systems and have not acquired the prejudices of longer term employees. These stars may be viewed as threats to their immediate managers and workers. They are saying and doing things that frustrate a lot of other employees. The other employees' frustration grows out of the fact that they, too, tried when they were new to the company. But minus a system in place to make it happen, nothing will change. The new employee will soon be brought down to the level of the old.

In my program, that star is provided a system which allows them to step up and shine. Stars may come from many places. We've had them step up from the secretarial position, from manufacturing, from production, from management, and even the truck drivers and the service department.

There are great people within any organization. When they see an opportunity and system in place to make things happen, the stars will rise. They will take this program and do their best to make things happen. You will see the organization change from a dictatorial management system to a system where everyone possesses a hands-on team member attitude. The quality program coordinator (oftentimes a star) becomes strength within the organization. That star from within is given the tools to make change.

Now, you might be asking yourself the question, "Why don't the human resource department personnel coordinate the quality program, since they are responsible for training?" Well, that's a good question!

The human resource people are usually powerless to do that because they are somewhat abused in relation to their sphere of responsibility. In today's world of business, they get involved in risk management, hazardous waste issues, and many other things that have them doing everything except human resources. In many places, the companies have lost sight of what their human resource employees are supposed to do. Most human resource directors are as overworked as other employees.

The stars at the beginning of the program, again, are the employees who don't have a defeated attitude and really want to get things done. Most employees start out this way, but because of the lack of systems necessary for change, they are discouraged and soon fall into that shut-down employee mode.

> #50 *Even though the sky of an organization is full of stars, they will never shine without the commitment and direction of leadership.*

OK, LET'S START !

Story #51

Most organizations never start the change process, because they don't know where to begin. How do we change corporate culture? How do we change how we're doing business? Where do we start?

These are all valid questions. I got started by coming to the realization that quality wasn't needed in just one particular area; it was required in every business process and step.

If we go to one workcenter, we will find problems elsewhere. We just end up putting our fingers in the many holes in the dike. Also, when there is no system or program in place, we find ourselves going in circles chasing our tails. My program knows that the majority of the problems in an organization are due to lack of communication (verbal and written) and/or implied procedures. So we start with the BaseWork Centers, with procedures, with the four barriers to quality. That's how we get started. No other program out there answers these questions. There has not been a tool or system, until mine, BaseWork Systems 2000, for the CEO or management to implement a quality improvement program such as this.

Corporate America is spending billions a year on training, so we know they are trying. But regardless of this expenditure, I believe the training industry has suffered from the lack of a tool to provide change within an organization. It just can't be in a single area like secretarial, management, manufacturing, upper management, etc. **It must be across the board**. The whole company has to be heading in one direction, talking the same terminology. When that is happening, we know where everybody is going to end up. That's how we start.

#51 *There is never an ideal time for an organization to start the implementation of a quality program, just start.*

RETAINING THE FOUNDERS PERSONALITY

Story #52

Over time, a company loses the personality of its founder. The founder, as a person, is responsible for making the organization what it is. Even when you are talking about a Fortune 500 Company, there is little difference. Most of our great companies were founded by individuals and families who possessed great integrity and commitment to do what was right. As these companies grow, the founder starts hiring people, then they start hiring other people, and on it goes, until the founder has less interaction with employees on a day-to-day basis. The faster the growth the worse it gets. The company may have tremendous growth in sales and out of necessity, must hire numerous people to handle it. The founder now works at holding everything together.

When a company has between $23 and $27 million in sales, it has to formalize how it is doing business. All of a sudden the business has gotten too big for the CEO to manage alone. He can no longer handle everything.

The department walls and barriers rise because of hidden agendas. Conflict between jobs, departments, and divisions starts. Many people have their own agendas and want to keep it the way it is because it's safe. They know what's expected, they know how to survive, and they don't want to correct and improve because it's just easier not to.

As this goes on, we see employees saying they like the CEO, but they don't like the company anymore. The CEO has lost touch! The personality that made the company what it is and the strength behind it has been lost in the day-to-day running of the business.

The four barriers to quality start to become evident at this point. The founder sits shaking his head wondering how he can move the company to the next level. How can he pass this legacy on, if he can't handle the issues himself?

Losing the personality and character of the founder is very common in most organizations and is also very sad. The founders may start to get short-tempered when inundated by questions, problems, and recommendations. The owner may realize that he can't do anything about the overall nature of the business because there isn't a system set up to handle it. He might delegate it to his management, but they aren't prepared, nor do they have the tools to handle it.

The toughest thing is to try to get back the personality of the founder and the corporate structure. Without a good systemic approach, it just won't happen.

> #52 *Growth without formalizing the way we do business, is a sure fire way to lose the personality of the founder of the organization.*

A TOOL FOR FAMILY SUCCESSION

Story #53

Some time back, about a year as I remember, it was brought to my attention by a very good friend and business associate that he would like to pass down the family business to his children. He told me about a seminar he attended at a college that talked about transferring ownership of a business from one generation to the next.

The presenter said that most people in business have the majority of their money tied up in the business and don't have liquid assets. Also, most don't feel comfortable with their heirs taking the company and running it.

The only way to give their children something is to sell the company, but they don't really want to do that because they have put their lives and hearts into it. Most founders tell their children to get out and learn the business, but the children turn around and say how?

They may send their children to a vice president within the company and tell him to train their children. But the vice president may not want to do this because he wants to ultimately take over the company. He certainly doesn't want the child of an owner looking over his shoulder.

The children feel frustrated because they know they could never work as hard or be as good as their parents. They have low self-esteem.

My position is that since most parents want to give the business to their children, we should communicate to them the proper procedure. Children shouldn't feel guilty that their parents want to give the business to them—that's simply the natural order of things.

Fathers and mothers want to build an organization to pass on so that their children will have an advantage. Children need to accept that.

If you, as a child, are concerned what the employees think about your stepping into the company, then you are worried about the one percenters. What you will find is that many of the employees want the children to come in and take over, because most of the time the children have the same integrity as the founder and they have great compassion for the employees. Typically, the children have worked throughout the business over the years and have personal relationships with many of the employees.

My friend made the observation that most of the companies that I had dealt with were family owned and operated. To pass the business on to the heirs is a significant tax issue. He said my program is less expensive than tax.

The business owner has the dilemma of what to do and how to go about it. My program can and has facilitated the transition from founders to heirs. And, yes, this program is cheaper than tax, and a lot more fun!

> #53 *With training, direction, and the right tools, most children of the founders can lead the organization into the next generation.*

FLAT ORGANIZATIONS (SELF MANAGERS)

Story #54

By defining our BaseWork Centers, we become a flat organization. What I mean by flat is that there are no layers of management or structure between the man on the floor and the man on the top.

Quality will not cost jobs but create new ones. We are not saying get rid of management. Management is another line-item issue that's easy to cut, their jobs will not be cut but they will change.

Everyone's job will somewhat change and become more focused. We may have three managers in a given area. We are not going to get rid of them. Rather their jobs will be more specifically defined, and therefore, the manager will become more effective and more focused. That manager's job might change from basic management to being more focused on data analysis, or on his department's day-to-day operations.

When we say we don't need quality inspectors, we're not saying we need to fire the inspectors; we're saying their jobs will become more defined and focused. We can't expect quality out of the process right from the beginning. We must first improve the process.

When the organization focuses on the four barriers, it will become a flat, self-managed organization with the BaseWork Centers managing themselves and holding each other accountable. Remember, we should be able to walk up to anybody in the organization and ask an open and honest question and get an open and honest answer. That's what it means to have flat organization. As a result, the companies will become more efficient.

> #54 *A quality organization moves from management holding employees accountable for quality to employees being responsible and personally accountable. They don't pass on or accept non-quality. This means that, in effect, employees are now holding one another accountable for quality in every process, step, procedure and system in that organization.*

DEPARTMENTAL WALLS

Story #55

Departmental walls form within a company when departments are forced to compete with one another. It happens because there is strong expectation from above, for all areas to nail their numbers.

For example, it doesn't really bother me if I'm in accounting, and manufacturing is having a problem. As long as I meet my numbers and quota, that's all I care about. When one department questions another, we see the departmental walls coming up. The reason for this is that most organizations have no defined systems or processes to handle conflict.

Manufacturing is upset when accounting says their numbers are wrong and accounting is upset with manufacturing saying they aren't doing the correct paperwork. The walls go up so long as the budget and quotas are being independently assigned to departments. It doesn't matter how the walls affect the overall operation.

It does, however, affect the whole organization. That's what happens when we start setting quotas without defining how we are doing business or putting other planning vehicles into place.

Let's say we have a salesman who is out doing his job. The market says we need product x and y. So the salesman goes back and explains this to his manager. The sales manager says that's great, but the numbers and the budget have been forecasted to sell 1,000 of product x only. He tells his salesman to go out and sell 1,000 of product x.

Eventually this manager is held responsible for the market and his sales quota to a vice president who tells him that sales are down and the budget isn't being met. The sales manager goes back to his salesman and complains. The salesman comes back and says that he did what he was told.

The production manager's "wall" is that he was committed to building 1,000 of product x, and he doesn't have the budget to retool for something else. He even goes so far as to explain a past experience where he responded to a hair-brain idea and ended up getting in trouble. His expenses went up 15% and he ended up dumping it.

The reason the above scenario happens is because a knee-jerk forecast was made and had little to do with hard data. Accurate marketing research data could have saved a lot of problems.

Instead, the walls start forming. The Vice President of Manufacturing, the Vice President of Sales and the Sales Manager's defenses are rising. They may have lost 20% of the market over an 18-month period, and the President of the organization is screaming that sales must come up. Everyone starts pointing fingers in different directions and manufacturing gets blamed.

Manufacturing responds by defending their position saying they have to retool. They can't retool because the Vice President of the division has committed to a budget. Everyone is afraid and placing the blame elsewhere because the issue wasn't addressed 18 months ago. If the company had formed a task team or developed a format to solve the problems, this never would have gotten out of control.

Now we go through the retooling but don't meet budget and everyone is upset. The walls are all up between manufacturing, sales, vice presidents and salesmen. All the salesmen are trying to do is sell the product. All the customer wants is the product they need. You can easily see how departmental walls build up with hidden agendas and quotas and then communication gets shut down.

#55 Departmentally, quotas and incentives usually build departmental walls which become barriers to quality. They do this by creating competition from one department to the other, resulting in one department winning and another losing. The ultimate loser is going to be the customer as well as the company's long-term client base.

RESOLVING NEGATIVE ATTITUDES

Story #56

One of the big interpersonal problems within many organizations has to do with negative attitudes. This spreads like a cancer. Many times we communicate in our day-to-day life in negative ways. For example, walk up to somebody and tell them how terrible they look. That begins the process of one person hitting negatively on another and that person returns with another negative hit. We call this negative rap.

Negative attitude is a disease in an organization. People will say it is done in jest or fun, but mentally many people can't separate what is fun and what is meant to be harmful or negative. The mind can't make that decision so it registers as a negative. Pretty soon we get a lot of negative energy built up inside, then BOOM! We blow up at what somebody only meant as a joke. Because we can't take any more, they set us off. The result is a conflict between two employees. Remember, people remember seven negatives over one positive.

When we look at things with a negative attitude, we look at life from the worst side. When we look at life positively, we look at the situations and wonder how we can build it and make it better.

A negative attitude eats at a person internally. When there is a negative attitude at work, it doesn't stay there. It goes home with that person. It can't be turned off and on even though we say it can.

My program trains people to do away with the negative attitude by getting up in the morning and making a conscious effort to think positive and say to themselves that they're going to have a good day. It is totally our decision and we mentally make the choice to have the best or the worst of a day.

If you wake up and your spouse says you don't look good, it's almost guaranteed you'll have a bad day. That negative attitude becomes a part of you. Then you go to work and you already feel beaten down. Your boss says good morning and you respond negatively. That's a negative attitude. That attitude is contagious and pretty soon that's the only way you know how to communicate.

So, what we do is get the company to make a commitment that they are up, positive and concerned with one another. We must make a positive, happy attitude acceptable and encourage it. When you smile on the outside, something happens on the inside and you become that smile.

My position is that constant reinforcement is needed from management and everyone is expected to display a positive attitude. Believe it or not there are some poor souls that fight this tooth and nail, saying they can't be positive; they aren't like that.

Well, maybe we can't change them, but we can model a positive attitude for them. Also, we don't have to tolerate negative rap or negative attitude.

#56 *A positive company attitude is contagious and attracts customers.*

SMILE

Story #57

Because of the negative rap and vibes that are not only in our companies but in our communities, we made a law about being positive and supportive of one another. It's okay to smile and say hello to your co-worker. It's okay to ask, "How are you doing. Is there anything I can do to help out?" We call this *"SMILE"* (a **S**mile in the **M**orning **I**mproves **L**ife **E**veryday). The first half-hour at work sets the tone for the rest of the day.

Management struggles with how to start conversations and get the positive communication going. We just said, "Say **SMILE**." You can imagine the response we got. Everyone was laughing and giggling and saying, "**SMILE**." As you might suspect, a lot of people used it in a negative, demeaning way to upset one another.

Maybe someone was having a bad day and putting out fires and a fellow employee throws at him "**SMILE**." You get some of that. When we started it in class, everybody started laughing, especially the big macho guys. But the company has to walk the walk and talk the talk.

What happened at first when we used the term and said, "**SMILE**" was that everyone laughed and started talking with each other. But in about six months, we no longer had to use the term because there was no need. The communication was positive and upbeat, with people smiling at each other. People no longer seemed to have a problem talking to each other. We no longer needed the simple icebreaker as a tool, but were now communicating and getting positive reinforcement and feeling good about our jobs and one another.

That first half hour sets the tone for the day. During that time we have the freedom to make a conscious decision to have either a good day or bad day. It's tough enough coming to work day in and day out. Let's have as good a time as possible and be happy.

The company helps make that decision for its employees by setting the example and using this tool from the top down. You can't be positive in sales and negative in manufacturing, or positive in manufacturing and negative in accounting. It just doesn't work. Every BaseWork Center and every job must be positive across the board.

> #57 *A good positive attitude in the morning sets the tone for a good positive work day.*

TAKE IT AS A WIN

Story #58

One of the things that I have discovered is that we dwell on the negative things in our lives and store them up. But when we have a win, we discount it and move on. Our problem is that we don't step back and take account of our wins.

One of the examples that I use is a boy going out and playing baseball. His father is in the stands watching because it's a big game. The young man hits a home run. The team is all excited because they win the game. The son comes home, but doesn't see his father right after the game. Later the boy asks, "Dad, Dad, did you see me hit that home run?" "Well, yes I did son, but you struck out three times." That negativism takes the wind right out of his sails. Instead of looking at the positive he dwelt on the negative. Here is this young boy looking for affirmation, acceptance and a win and, instead, he gets a blow to his self-esteem and ego. The older we get, the more it becomes a part of us and becomes tougher to change. Here, he had a win but was confronted with the negative. He'll remember seven negatives for every one positive.

The negative is fear. Usually a negative thing has a negative effect on us and the positive doesn't. We have more tendency to worry about the negative side, which I believe in turn makes us focus on the negative rather than the positive.

Examples: "I did a good job at work today. No one patted me on the back." Pat yourself on the back. Or, someone says to you, "You did a great job." Respond by saying, "Well, thank you and I would agree, I did do a good job." Don't turn it around and say, "Well, the only reason I finished early is because I had some good luck." That's negative rap, again.

We have this feeling we must justify in a negative way, rather than accept the positive as a win. We do not take enough account of our wins as we go through life. We need to focus on the positives and relish those positive moments. Discard the negative and move on. Don't let the negative become baggage you continue to carry around.

> #58 *Take daily accounts of your wins and discard the negatives. We have a tendency to discount our wins and focus on the negatives.*

PROBLEMS AT HOME AND AT WORK

Story #59

Most people feel there is an unspoken rule—leave your personal problems at home and your professional problems at work. Some people believe they can do that. I have never seen a situation where someone that is having a really bad day at work can simply shut it off and go home. If an employee doesn't like his supervisor or is having problems with a co-worker, then it becomes very difficult not to reflect that negative attitude at home.

The same is true at work if a person is having problems with his marriage or children at home. That's why we need a balance in our lives. That balance oftentimes starts with open and honest communication both at work and home.

If we are having a tough time at home, then we need somebody to whom we can talk. Most of the people to whom we can talk daily are those with whom we work. If the rule at work is to leave your problems at home, those internal struggles will constantly build and eat away at the employee. It can make him bitter, angry, and ultimately cause shut-down, which in turn affects his relationship with co-workers, which in turn interferes with work.

We try to teach in my program BaseWork Systems 2000 that people need to care for one another in the company. Everyone goes through problems. Be that someone that helps a colleague out at work. If you know someone is having a bad day, then ask if there is anything he needs to talk about, or maybe just go have lunch with him.

Compassion is a gift we offer one another. We don't need to always solve everybody else's problems. The greatest thing they may need is a good listener. Once they air their difficulties, it will lighten them up.

I have had the same thing happen to me when I have a bad day or lose a customer. When I come home, my baby and wife sense it immediately, even if I try to cover it up and say there isn't anything wrong and that I had a great day. I may try to shut it off, but it does affect my home life. That's why we need open communication with our spouse as well as with people at work. My program teaches a process to resolve these issues. If we are communicating at work, working at solving problems, and it's done correctly, when we're done, we are able to go home and talk to our spouse about it.

When we hold it in, then it creates stress that assaults us and may even bring on illness. Stress, as you know, weakens the immune system. If we examined the facts, we would find that stress is becoming one of the top causes of illness. It causes a breakdown in the natural processes of our body and robs us of our strength and ability to fight off illness.

There's an old saying, "Get it off your chest and you'll feel better." There is great truth in those few words. Communication is imperative for our physical and mental health. We need to promote the use of this vehicle both at work and at home.

People should offer a helping hand to fellow employees who are having problems at home and help them through the crisis. Eventually we all go through things in life with which we'll need help and understanding.

If we spend the greatest amount of time at work, we need the opportunity to open up and express ourselves and move on. People that move from one tragedy to the next are surrounded by negative energy and this will rob them of a happy, fulfilling life.

> #59 *Be the first worker to step up and show compassion, concern and respect for your fellow employee.*

OPEN AND HONEST COMMUNICATION

Story #60

One of the things we talk about and put in writing up front is that we want open and honest communication. That means that anyone in the company can walk up to anybody with a legitimate, open and honest question and expect to get an open and honest answer. I feel that is the base and the foundation of my program. That helps remove the fear and opens the communication necessary for solving most of the problems within an organization.

If you could look at our government and politics and see open and honest communication, it would make a major difference to our country. If you could walk up to the CEO and say, "This is a problem and we need to do this to solve it," most of our problems could be solved simply.

The problem is that we don't really have open communication; typically, what we have is filtered communication. There are many people that take bits and pieces of information that sound legitimate, and because they are smart, change the information just a little bit and make it a half-truth or a lie that best fits their situation. To the person receiving it, a manager or the CEO, it sounds correct. We need to be very careful that we communicate truthfully and honestly. We must treat one another with respect and dignity and present the issue without making personal attacks or exercising hidden agendas. It is very important to set the rules up front with open and honest communication throughout the organization.

#60 *An organization being open and honest with itself and its employees is an important step in* **breaking through the four barriers to quality.**

THE COMPANY RULE

Story #61

When we go into a company, we find the need for rules. As the employees and management start looking at the program, everyone tries to interpret what the company wants. This becomes very frustrating unless the rules and goals have been written down along with the BaseValues.

For example, if we are smiling, greeting one another, and having fun, we're reprimanded for goofing off. To prevent this, we have a company rule which states that we want the employees to be honest, open, happy, and caring for themselves and other employees.

We have two other rules which are very important and are the keys for the company's BaseValues: 1) do what is morally and ethically correct, and 2) treat everybody as you want to be treated. We find it important for the company to state in writing what they want and what they expect. If not, everyone will interpret it differently.

It's just like a procedure in a process or a system in manufacturing; we have to define it so everyone clearly understands it. So, if you want everyone to be honest, positive, happy, concerned about fellow employees, and treating one another with respect—put it in writing. It then sets the tone for our managers up front. We have twenty-two items on which the CEO signs off. The list of items functions as a checklist for success and speaks of their commitment.

> *#61* *A company's honesty and integrity cannot be left up to interpretation by its employees.*

TRUST

Story #62

One of the biggest problems in business today is a lack of trust; trust between employees and management, trust between management and unions, and trust between unions and the overall company. That's pretty much the way it has always been.

Given that trust is really important, how do we promote trust within an organization? One of the best ways is commit to it in writing. After that, just walk the walk and talk the talk. What I have learned from the four barriers—fear of expression or action, communication, written procedure, and training, is that consistency in management is the primary ingredient necessary for promoting trust. We must do what we say we're going to do, and we must follow up on it. We also have to treat everybody the same. Take attendance, for example. If one employee doesn't get away with a violation, while another does, that is disheartening to the whole organization and to all the employees. That is what promotes lack of trust and creates fear.

If you are consistent, do what is morally and ethically correct, and treat everybody as you want to be treated, you get results. Don't put it in a memo and pin it up on a bulletin board or give a pep talk about it, then go back and do business as usual.

Even though my program is only 74 hours of training per employee, it takes 24 months. If you want to promote trust, then you must hold each other responsible, and be accountable, while working on the four barriers to quality. Without trust, you won't experience positive results and will end up with employees who fear you.

#62 *Trust cannot be bought; it has to be earned day in and day out by every employee within the organization. Trust is the foundation for change.*

BEING A GOOD NEIGHBOR

Story #63

My experience has been that, given an opportunity, most people will rally around and help another person in need. Take natural disasters as an example. They happen every year in many communities. People can be neighbors and never talk to one another, but if a tornado tears off a porch or roof, everyone is outside seeing if they can help others. People volunteer their home for shelter and gladly offer food, water, and clothing. People have a common cause or reason to reach out and help. Most people will help because they are very good people.

Given an opportunity in a company, people will also demonstrate that they are good neighbors. If management or another employee asks an employee to help out and improve a procedure, the response is usually very positive. When being asked for help, employees feel a bigger part of the company.

We are now starting to empower our employees by allowing them to help us with what they do best. Remember my rules; do what is morally and ethically correct and treat everybody as you want to be treated. We need to give people opportunities to show their true character and let them shine. The company must lead and give direction.

If you, the manager, walk into a conference room and ask if anybody has a quarter for a soda, your employees will buy you that soda and feel good about doing it. In a simplistic way, you have given the employees the opportunity to help their manager. It makes them feel good.

#63 Given the opportunity to help, people will help one another.

WE ALL WANT TO BELONG

Story #64

When I went to school and was not participating in sports, I felt as though I did not belong. As a result, I didn't have a real interest in school. My mother encouraged me, with some help from the principal, to work harder. I was successful. If not for this, I probably would have failed.

In the ninth grade, when I started participating in sports, I now felt I had a reason to go to school. In order to participate in sports, I had to get good grades. That rule motivated me to work harder.

I got a lot of gratification and self-esteem from sports in high school and junior college. I had a desperate need to belong during those years. Without sports to fill the need, I probably would have dropped out of school.

There is an analogy here for all the current gang activity. Most gang members want to belong. In their neighborhoods, there aren't many options, usually just one, belonging to a gang. Whereas, I wanted to belong to a sports team—they want to belong to a gang. They become a part of something and feel value in belonging.

Most people out of high school, or even college, don't have much sense of belonging anymore. If there is a lack of communication, they don't feel they belong to the company where they work. If there is communication, then it can work the opposite way.

When away from the company, you will oftentimes hear people saying good things about their company, maybe even wearing a company T-shirt or hat. But if that company is negative internally, and an employee is getting harassed every time they do something positive for the company, they'll shut- down and there won't be

225

communication. When an employee is involved, he feels like he belongs to the company.

Most people have their work and their homes and not much else. Many people work 10 hours a day and don't have time to get involved in outside activities. So given an opportunity, an employee will give their heart to a company. The company, however, must promote an environment worthy of that dedication. People want to belong.

#64 *Wanting to belong is not an option; it is a need.*

BILLY

Story #65

Billy represents an employee that has been given an opportunity to step out of his comfort zone and, with the support of the company, get involved in a quality program. When he first started with us, he was doing maintenance and clean-up work and would basically do anything he was asked to do. He worked unlimited hours, never complained, and was a dedicated, hard-working employee thankful that he had a job. As the program grew within the company, there were certain opportunities the program offered. Billy became one of the coordinators in the quality program. As the program matured, Billy took on more responsibilities and was one of our top people. He understood the overall program and had a good grasp of how it worked. He was a key to its success. He stepped up when it wasn't necessarily cool to be involved. Every company has a Billy that really wants to do well and make a difference and a change.

Later, as the program developed, it helped sharpen Billy's skills. He eventually left the company and went to another job where, from what we understand, he continues to do well. Billy is a perfect example of how the program can help somebody grow. By being involved in the program, the employee grows and gets a tremendous amount of benefit. They can then move to the next level of their potential.

> #65 *When given the opportunities, leaders will surface and rise to the occasion.*

THE GUY EVERYONE DISLIKES

Story #66

This is a good example of what some companies go through. There is a client of mine that I have known through the years. They started a quality program. In doing this, there were a lot of things in conflict. They had a Mission Statement about the company's current position, what it was doing, and where it was headed. The statement also talked about focusing on the customers and employees.

You know what? It was one of the worst environments I had ever seen in a company of that size. They had been involved in a quality program for a few years. When I asked one of the employees how many problem-solving steps they had in their process, he said he didn't know. I asked if they solved problems. He didn't know that. I asked how long the program had been going on and he said two years. I told him not to take my next question wrong but, "What do you know?" He said whenever he was late for a meeting it cost him a dollar. Here is a person who has been in the program for two years and doesn't have any idea what is going on in the program. The company has spent an extreme amount of money on the program and their Board commends themselves on the quality and the employee involvement.

The truth was, the employees weren't even plugged into the program. The reason they weren't plugged in was because of the fear; much of their middle and upper management were some of the most uninformed I have ever seen—telling the Board exactly what they wanted to hear. It was laid out plain and clear—you don't interact with upper management, the Board, or else.

For instance, there was one manager who everyone disliked. He was a department head who kept moving up in the company.

He was the perfect example of a bad employee that back-stabs and is not a good performer, yet knows how to brown-nose and move up the ladder.

One time I had to do business with him. Even though I had done a lot of work for the company, this man was extremely rude to me. We were in a meeting and had been working on a project for about six months. We had to have 14 people agree on the project, including him.

Well, we had a meeting to get the required signatures. Everyone at the table signed. This guy's power play was to always come to a meeting late. He always had meetings and phone calls to make and everybody was just shaking their head at what a terrible person he was. Everyone had signed this document but him. He came in late and refused to sign off and walked out without any explanation. Do you know that document went all the way around the table again and everybody that had signed it, erased their name from it. Tell me that's not fear. Thirteen people had signed off and one person didn't. During the next few days he came back and signed the deal, but he showed who had power and control.

This man was involved in many other things over which he had total control. He made sure the dice rolled his direction so that he could personally benefit from them at whatever cost. It would be interesting to investigate and find out just how much this one employee/manager cost the company, not to mention what he had personally gained by deception, hidden agendas, and selfish decision-making. He continued to get promoted. It was one of the saddest things I ever saw in a corporate structure.

This is a perfect example of how a little kingdom can be built that destroys an organization. The original owner had been ousted and everything was sold off a couple of times. Everyone made money— but the shareholders and the employees. This man would sit and look at his department, and, based on how many employees were under him, he would receive a pay raise. He built the number of people under him so he could get a raise. He manipulated the system. It had nothing to do with the organization, but only with his own self-gain and what he needed to do to get a raise.

> #66 *The bigger the organization, the less likely you are to consistently bump into that 1% bad employee within the organization. This gives that 1% employee the opportunity to wreak havoc on your organization. Employees must be encouraged to hold one another accountable and supported for their efforts.*

FAMILY SUCCESSION

Story #67

When there are children involved in a company their parents own, many unique characteristics are present. The children often have awkward feelings because their parent was the strong entrepreneur who worked hard to build the company. Oftentimes, they feel guilty since they haven't had to work as hard to get the benefits.

Children may feel awkward and insecure because they have the opportunity to take over the company. They realize there are employees who might be looking at them critically thinking they are lazy and that they are getting something for nothing. The strong parent/entrepreneur doesn't have time to train the successor/children in the business the way they need to be trained. Most of them delegate this to a vice president or somebody directly under them.

These managers don't want to see the children take over the company and so, directly or indirectly, they feed back to the entrepreneur that they don't feel the children have what it takes to make it. Upon hearing this, the entrepreneur gets frustrated and demonstrates his lack of confidence to the children. This continues to erode his children's self-esteem.

One of the things this program does is teach the children the business. They learn every system, process, procedure, and employee in the organization. They learn first-hand about the problems. The employees get to see them up close and personal, while learning something about their personalities and sincerity. Before you know it, the employees are rallying around these individuals. They really want the children to take over the company, because they know them and know they are good people.

One thing we teach the children is that every entrepreneur who has ever built a business wants to pass it down to his children. They want their children to have life easier. I've asked these children what they want to give to their children, and of course, they want to give them the same thing their parents wanted to give them. When they look at it from that aspect, they get a different feeling about their parents. They know it is okay to have a leg up on everybody else. That's why the entrepreneur built the company.

We also tell them it's okay to take over the family business, because they deserve it. It's their parents' business and they deserve to have it easier. The employees may say they are spoiled. My response to that is, they may be talking bad about you, but do they really know you? Should we be concerned with what they are saying?

The children need to believe in themselves, know they are good people, and understand that the business is rightfully theirs and they deserve it. The parents have worked hard all these years to have something to give to the next generation.

My program teaches them to feel good about themselves, to feel good that the parent has worked hard to put the children in their current position. The children may also want to give something of value to their children someday. It's okay to inherit. Feel good about yourself. Have a great attitude and know you have the strength and the power to do well.

The BaseWork Systems 2000 teaches children the business. It helps them build the good relationships with the organization that are necessary for successful succession.

> #67 *The hardest thing in regard to succession planning in the BaseWork Systems 2000 is the parent letting go of the business and letting his children assume the day-to-day responsibilities.*

JOE

Story #68

Joe was hired by the President of an organization to go in and develop a database for a particular division. Joe went in, worked hard, and did well. When the President flew in to meet with his friends, Joe was included. After awhile, they all became friends.

In the interim, a new general manager came in and began to go to these events. He, however, wasn't accepted by the President's friends. They liked Joe better.

Joe could see resentment from this new general manager building up because of Joe's relationship with the President. The general manager began putting a lot of land mines in Joe's way. He started spreading rumors that Joe drank and partied too much. He stated he wasn't intelligent enough to do the business and the only reason he was there was because of the President of the company.

At the same time, Joe was putting in a lot of hours on his assigned project. He was really beginning to shine. Because his project was going so well, Joe was asked to duplicate and develop it for other offices within the company.

That really upset the general manager. The general manager complained about having to pay Joe, and said he should be paid from the corporate office. He was negative and unsupportive. As Joe went to the other divisions, the rage began to build up in the general manager. He moved Joe into sales. Immediately, he took him off the draw and was hoping Joe would leave. Joe persevered.

After several days, the general manager told Joe he wasn't smart enough or good enough to do the job. He fired Joe!

Even though Joe had only worked three weeks in sales, he had completed a deal for which he should have received a sizeable commission. The general manager wouldn't hear of it and told him they didn't owe him the commission and that if he wanted it, he would have to sue for it.

Joe was not in a position to sue and wanted to put all the negative activities behind him. He didn't pursue it; he parted company like a gentleman.

The general manager obviously lacked Joe's level of integrity. Additionally, he lacked any sort of measurable skills in managing people. Here was an employee who was working hard and doing a great job. The manager, however, was jealous and saw him as a threat.

This is a good example of how a great employee can be run out of an organization. Joe found out later that the general manager had spread rumors to the other employees that he was going to be fired. The employees wouldn't say anything to him because of their relationship with Joe and their fear of losing their jobs.

Joe went to another company and within a year exceeded all industry expectations. Within two years, he had done better than anybody else in the industry and had proven he could do what the general manager said he would never achieve.

This general manager left the company. We don't know what he is doing, but we do know that Joe is the leader in that industry. He may have lost the battle, but he won in the long run.

This is a sad example of how an employee can be defeated, not because he can't perform his work, but because of personal conflicts, jealousy, insecurity and of being managed by a person who does not know how to handle employees. A lot of relationships end up this way.

The President had no inkling of what was going on, except through information given to him directly or indirectly by the general manager. There are many people that share this same kind of story.

> #68 *The integrity of your organization may not be reflected daily by your boss, so don't judge your organization too harshly.*

EMPLOYEES HOLDING THE COMPANY HOSTAGE

Story #69

When I say an employee holds a company hostage, I mean the employee uses threats to exercise power over the company. The company then goes into panic mode at the prospect of losing the person or having to shut down because of a problem.

When we formalize the way we are doing business within the organization, often times we hear comments from the salesmen such as, "Do you want me to come to the meeting rather than service my customer?" No, what we want them to do is schedule the meeting so they can service the customer around that meeting time. If they are so worried they'll lose their customers, my question to them is, why? Are they not doing the preparation to ensure a positive relationship with that customer? Sometimes within the sales force, accountability, managing, and monitoring are ignored because the person has been performing well. We just let him slide and overlook his short comings. He doesn't get his time cards in on time;, his account billings are late; he doesn't do his monthly statements; he doesn't do his prospecting like he should or doesn't turn in his records.

We let him go because we have other people who are not performing at his level. Gradually, he does his own thing. He may be a top performer, but he cannot go out and represent the company in a real quality fashion. He's not good at paperwork, so if we tell him he's responsible for that, he'll quit. We all rush to work through his problems. Soon he learns how to manipulate the company because of his good accounts.

This is what we call holding the company hostage. We're in a mad rush to dance around the employee that is threatening us. With this behavior, he sets a very bad tone for other employees. As we try to develop our sales force and bring them in through training and this new system, they see our top salesman ignoring it all. How do you think that new salesman in training is feeling?

The top salesman has manipulated everybody because of his success. The company is jumping through hoops. If that person wants to leave, he'll leave after a time, no matter how we try to please him.

My question to the company is, why are they so afraid of losing this employee? The reason is because we don't know enough about his job, his accounts, or his customers. That shows we have no control over our business.

Another example of an employee holding the company hostage is the one percent that are negative and doing everything wrong by manipulating the system, hidden agendas, and double standards. We are in meetings spending time talking about these bad employees. If we fire him, or make him accountable, he will sue us or he'll end up shooting or killing somebody.

I have found that if the employee is going to sue, he'll do so regardless of how we try to work around him. If we don't hold him accountable, all he is doing is building his database to support his case. If we don't document his missing work or coming in late and we fire him, we go to court without documentation. Guess who the judge is going to believe?

We must hold everybody accountable and have good documentation. The employee can hold us hostage if we don't! He will have a strong case against us and we will have a weak one. While we sit on pins and needles over this one employee, our other employees are insulted by the treatment this guy is getting and what he gets away with.

Once we bring in our quality program and introduce accountability, things can be set up correctly with good monitoring of the systems. There will be no hidden agendas or past prejudices about how bad this individual is. The company **will hold everybody accountable** for the policies and procedures.

The next example of an employee holding the company hostage is the employee who has been doing his job so long that no one else really knows what he is doing. The knowledge of and information about this job is not written down. Once we start putting the systems and processes into place, this employee complains he's been doing the job for 25 years. Why are they now asked to follow the program. They get angry and threaten to leave. The company gets frightened that they'll lose this valued employee, so they start dancing around his demands. Again, it creates the double standards and the hidden agendas. He has learned to manipulate his knowledge and expertise so he gets around what's being asked of him.

If you are so afraid of losing him, then you have no control over that particular process or individual. You don't do certain things because you're afraid he's going to quit. If he's been with the company for a long period of time, then he likely won't leave. When it comes down to it, he will fall into line. If this employee has seen a bunch of programs start and end, he probably thinks this is just another "program of the month." His attitude may be negative at the onset, but when he sees the company being consistent, he will come around.

Maybe an employee is claiming injury and is saying he's going to go out on workmen's compensation or a medical leave. If he is really going to do it, nothing we do can stop him. Where we are most vulnerable is when we are not processing the information properly and documenting exactly what has happened. If the man's back is hurting, send him to a doctor. The longer we wait, the worse it gets. The natural threat will be, "If you don't let me have time to rest and heal my back, I will have to go out on a medical leave and be out for six months." This leads to him taking sporadic days off and upsetting the other employees with his hidden agendas.

This is, again, what we call holding the company hostage. This can happen with top management as well as with the average employee. We have to be conscious about how we handle the situation. We must document how we do business and formalize our processes and systems. Above all, we must do the right thing.

A word of caution when we talk about an employee holding a company hostage: Remember our rule that 99% of our employees are good people and want to do a good job. We have to go into it with that attitude. A poor employee's past history may be the company's fault. If he wasn't being monitored, or documented, or the systems weren't in place, then it's the company's responsibility. We have to drive a stake in the ground and move forward holding everybody accountable from that time on.

We don't go in with a vendetta or a hidden agenda with this person. We simply set the rules; we explain that it's the company's fault that this person has been out of control, and it is our responsibility to bring that employee around and get him focused.

Remember, it is only one to five percent of the employees holding the company hostage. Four percent will fall into line once we start the system and process. The one percent will raise its ugly head and leave. Let's remember that as we're going through the program.

#69 *The best way to deal with an employee that is holding the company hostage is to remove all emotion, and manage, monitor, and hold him accountable. This employee will process himself out.*

BEING ACCOUNTABLE
FOR QUALITY

Story #70

Sometimes we get into the position where we are trying to manage and monitor everything in an organization as a management team. What I have discovered is that we can't begin to hire enough managers to do that. That's why most of our management runs from one fire to another. That's why when we talk about holding each other accountable, it's not just management holding management accountable or holding the employees accountable; its employees holding employees accountable.

A lot of conflict within an organization has to do with people not being held accountable. I don't mean this in a negative way because many times we don't really know what the jobs are or what we're responsible for, so how can we be held accountable?

We must break down the organization by jobs or BaseWork Centers within the organization. We don't accept or pass on non-quality. What we do accept is what we agreed on as quality. Even though we don't accept non-quality, we don't attack; we simply work at resolving the issues. This comes back to holding everybody accountable, including the owner of the company. There can be no double standard with this. That will be in conflict with the policies and procedures.

If the managers/employees get upset, it is unacceptable. How do we address it? As a quality issue, that's how. Again, everyone has to be held accountable. The only way that can be done is to hold each other accountable. The only way we can do this is to agree on what constitutes our jobs, processes, systems and BaseWork Centers. We then formalize the way we do business and train our employees on it.

So now instead of having 100 employees and 10 managers that are managing, we have 100 employees managing and 100 quality whistleblowers. Non-quality will no longer be accepted from anybody. We have to hold each other accountable. When you start doing this, your employees will write tougher procedures and policies and be more accountable than you ever thought possible.

We were in a training class and somebody came up and said, "Bruce, we just went over this policy the other day in regard to paperwork. Our top salesman came in with only half the required paperwork. He was told we couldn't accept it and he blew up. He went to the President of the company and complained that we're keeping him from doing his job. He claimed he would lose his client if he's forced to do his paperwork. The President responded that he would take care of it."

This is where double standards click in to the process. We might as well not have policies and procedures if we can't manage and monitor everybody and hold one another accountable. This is where the conflict starts.

My question to the salesman is, "Did you not have training?" In my program a procedure does not go into practice without the proper paperwork and the training. So, evidently he must have conveniently missed the training. So now he must be trained on the procedure and held accountable.

We have actually had an owner come in conflict with a policy. He argued that he owned the company and asked if we were trying to tell him how to run it. "No, we are not trying to do that. What we are doing, is what we agreed on, and now we have to hold everybody accountable. It is unfair to ask an employee for anything different. He agreed with a big smile.

The owner may say, "I'm the owner of the company; I want this department to do it for me this way." That puts the department in an awkward position and might put them behind on other customers' work orders.

So here again, the strong entrepreneur must learn to have trust in the process and procedures and his employees. The only reason he has done it the other way is because that's all he's ever known. Now we are building an organization for this CEO that will help him run his business and make his organization more efficient.

You must break through the four barriers to quality. Number one is fear. I can't hold that person accountable because I could get fired if I refuse to do what the owner asks me to do. Number two is lack of communication. Evidently someone is not communicating because the salesman and the owner don't want to follow procedures properly. Maybe they haven't had the training on that particular procedure or that procedure is incorrect or not in writing. You can see there are many things that keep a company from not hitting on all cylinders. Sometimes we're consistent and sometimes not. That is why accountability is so very important. You can't hold somebody accountable if they haven't been trained, the procedure is not in writing, or it hasn't been agreed on how the business is to operate. That's why open and honest communication is so important. There must be a strong desire to follow through on commitments, thus providing a basis of morality to which the company adheres. This equates to doing what is morally and ethically correct and treating everybody as you want to be treated.

The program position stresses that if we have addressed all **4 Barriers to Quality** and the answers are yes, then that person must be held accountable. There can be no personal attacks. We don't jump to conclusions. We deal with data and work in a rational fashion.

> #70 *Being and saying you are of quality and being held accountable for quality are two completely different things. You cannot be quality until you can hold quality accountable.*

BETTY

Story #71

Betty is an example of a frustrated but caring secretary who worked hard and did a good job. When the program started, she became very vocal and outspoken in the process. As it grew and developed, Betty started taking on additional responsibilities within the program. She became our coordinator.

Betty had been at the company for several years, but her talents weren't really being utilized. Basically, they weren't exposed. With the quality program, she had the opportunity. We discovered that her work and work ethic had been squashed by internal issues. Now she had an avenue to put her full potential to use (the program encourages that).

The owners of the company noticed the change and her job expanded. Before the program, she was a secretary and bookkeeper, but now her skills were highlighted and she could move up. The program allowed her strengths to be shown. She went from being frustrated to being a very happy employee content with her job.

She felt she owed a great deal to the program because it had given her an opportunity to step out and get involved, a chance to do the things she wanted to do. The lack of systems and processes made it too complicated before.

Betty developed one of our largest Task Teams which led to an $8,000 a month savings in the processing of the Purchase Orders. She is a perfect example of a shining star.

> #71 *That extraordinarily talented employee that you seek is probably already in your employment.*

WHERE DO WE START

Story #72

The toughest thing for the President/CEO is when he realizes he has problems within the organization, but doesn't know where to start solving them. Let's say he has a problem in manufacturing. Because there is no program in place, by the time he starts addressing that issue, he may see problems cropping up in sales. He tries to work through the problem in manufacturing, and guess what? He finds he isn't getting the right information from the Purchase Orders, an accounting problem. Or maybe the warehouse men aren't keeping accurate records as they pull production from the shelves. Can you see the CEO's problem? Of course you can! The initial problem has grown to be very complex and appears to be only the tip of the iceberg. What does he do now?

My research has found that most organizational problems are due to informal business structure. So, one of the first things we need to do is define the systems and the way in which we are doing business. Also, we need to look at the four barriers to quality: fear of expression and/or actions, lack of communication, lack of written procedures, and lack of training. This is where we start.

The entire company has to be involved in training for this transition. The BaseWork Systems 2000 operates on the premise that 98% of the problems are due to the four barriers to quality. Previously, most entrepreneurs jumped in and tried to do the best they could. That effort often involved buying individual training programs and attempting to make them work. Well, that doesn't work very well. Most off-the-shelf, canned, one-program-fits-all approaches aren't going in any one particular direction. That makes it really tough to get started. I find that most companies want to start with a training program and start addressing the issues. But what happens? As we're juggling everything else, training is the first ball to be dropped. This happens even though we keep saying this is what we need to do.

In defense of most CEO's out there, there really hasn't been a manageable tool that the CEO could implement within the company. The biggest problem with our decision-makers is they want to know how much, what they are going to end up with, and when. Well, that solution wasn't out there. A system was needed to attack the four barriers to quality. That's how my program was developed.

What we are able to do is go to the CEO with the following information: what it will cost, where we're going to start, where we're going to end up, and the time it's going to take. So for the first time, the CEO has a tangible product. We feel this is the only existing tool that the CEO can use to build business infrastructure.

#72 *The best way to get started training an organization is:*
1. *Make sure you are committed long term to training.*
2. *Budget 2%–6% of payroll for that training.*
3. *Plan and schedule your training a year in advance and hold everybody accountable.*

TRAINING DIRECTION

Story #73

One of the problems in most organizations is that training is non-directional. Trainers do not communicate or talk with one another. For example, if we're getting computer training, management training, and self-help training, who is coordinating it all?

The training is usually coming from different vendors with different ideas as to what the company needs. You can bet your bottom dollar they aren't talking among themselves. Why would they? They're probably competitors! I feel this is a real problem.

The training program is going in different directions. All we know is that we need training. The human resource and training department are trying to do the best they can to provide training based on what is available on the market.

When we look at the direction of training, it is an overpowering situation. Most companies have no solution regarding what the end product will be. They will continually turn that training dollar.

I believe most training in companies is inefficient, usually not job specific, and has no end in sight. The training direction is very important. We should never train just for the sake of training; we should always have long-term planning and scheduling. We must give direction to the training. Thirty-three percent inefficiency is the norm in organizations without systems definition and agreement.

BaseWork Systems 2000 gives direction to the training. This training affects every job, every system, every process, every procedure, and every department within that organization. It establishes a training budget and is perpetual, because it will continually build on itself, with the employees eventually administering it.

> #73 *The only way training within your organization will succeed is with the total commitment and sign off of the owner/President/CEO and Board. It will not happen any other way.*

CEO - LEADERSHIP

Story #74

When I go into a company and start addressing the four barriers to quality, and start looking at the systems, the processes, and the BaseWork Centers, a lot of people start getting defensive. They try to justify and defend their actions. The problem with this approach is that we spend 90% of the time defending or justifying why we do what we do. My program's position is that we don't care why or how problems were created. What we do care about is improving the company and defining the way it does business. We don't care who did what or why. What we want to do is figure out how to do it better. We take the negative energy required for defending and justifying and put it into defining problems and fixing the way we do business.

This approach clears the way for the CEO to sign a letter of commitment up front. In this letter, he talks about the problems and then personally accepts responsibility. If anyone wants to point blame, the finger can be pointed at the CEO. He alone has taken on this responsibility in the organization.

This loosens up a situation, because everyone now has broad shoulders upon which to lay the responsibility. Everyone lightens up and laughs about it. We now have team members reminding one another that the CEO has accepted this responsibility and we don't need to dwell on the current way business is being conducted.

You won't believe what starts happening next! People actually start defending the CEO saying it's not all his fault. They'll lay the blame where it should be. They demonstrate compassion for the boss by saying it's their problem. They've come to that conclusion and can now move through the issues, because it gives everybody a way out.

Remember, the intent is that we just want to improve the way we do business. We do not want to spend time, energy, or effort dwelling on why it got there or how. We want to spend that energy on fixing the problem and improving the way we are doing business.

So, in the very beginning, the CEO writes a letter and addresses the organization. He states, in writing, that whatever problems exist are his problems and he accepts full responsibility for them.

> #74 *The quickest way to get the program moving is for the owner/ President/CEO to step up and accept the responsibility and the burden for whatever is wrong in the organization. Now the company can move in a positive direction.*

EFFICIENT/EFFECTIVE TRAINING

Story #75

For a training program to be effective and efficient, it must be taken as seriously as any other job in the organization. Over the years, I have developed my own opinion of what is important and what is not important in training for quality. If taken seriously, it can and will improve any company.

At the very heart of my system is the need for every company in America to define the systems and processes within their organization. That in effect sets up the BaseWork Centers. The secret of the BaseWork Center process is that it requires that job procedures be written down and documented by the people that are doing the particular job everyday.

To have effective and efficient training, the plan must be well thought out and moving the entire company in one direction. That is why I believe the BaseWork Systems 2000 is the only effective base training program on the market. It encompasses the entire organization, affecting every job, every system, and every process in that organization.

Much of the training going on in companies is inefficient because it's non-directional. It's the flavor or program of the month. When we send people through the so-called training, a lack of systems and procedures defeats the training before they ever have time to use it. Oftentimes, training dollars are spent very inefficiently.

> #75 *For a training organization to be effective, everyone in that organization must receive job-specific training.*

QUALITY DIRECTOR

Story #76

What do you think when you hear the term, *Quality Director*? Most of us think it has to do with manufacturing, possibly the final inspection, or maybe we think it is inspecting quality into a product. Let's see if I can change your impression.

Most quality programs start off with good intentions. They usually end up, however, being in the business of quality auditing. If you're a quality auditor, you determine what passes and what doesn't pass. That's quite different from my definition of Quality Director.

The Quality Director should be improving the processes and systems so we don't need to inspect. Every time we inspect, we admit quality failure. We are trying to inspect quality into the program, when instead we should be building quality into the processes and systems of the organization.

I have seen big companies where the quality person goes around and says, "That's not quality." Or they determine if a department's payroll is too high. They could have had an accountant tell them that and save the money spent on a Quality Director.

Most Quality Directors never really improve the processes and systems for doing business, because there are no processes or systems. In that scenario, the quality person is the final inspector. Either it passes or it doesn't. Other quality people check the items as they come in from our suppliers.

Most Quality Directors are in engineering or manufacturing. Those aren't exactly the same. They're really two different jobs. An engineer is very specific and narrow in training. A good Quality Director needs to have skills of a much broader nature. They need awareness reaching into every department, not just engineering or manufacturing.

Quality awareness should be in every facet, system and process of the organization. You can't have continuing quality in manufacturing and not have it in the corporate office.

Do you ever notice how the local newspaper defines Quality Directors? They talk about inspectors. We need more than that. We need to build quality into the system, not merely attempt to inspect it into the product.

That's why my system doesn't accept or pass on non-quality products to the next level. In fact, everyone in the organization becomes his own quality inspector or own whistle blower. They don't accept or pass on non-quality.

Because of the four barriers, I believe one of the most important things in an organization is a Director of Quality, one that reaches into every department and division. Most human resource personnel, because of walls or barriers, can't go into a department without the defenses going up. This results in one department performing quality work and another not. Someone in the organization has to hold everybody accountable. The CEO/ President can't do it all.

So, we need a Quality Director or Coordinator that is responsible for holding everybody accountable. Let's not turn our quality people into final inspectors. Let's improve the processes and systems. Let's improve the way we are doing business.

A quality person may go through a plant or department and identify that something isn't quality. That's great. But he now must turn us around and show us how to get quality and how to improve our business. He also must address the four barriers, not just the systems and processes.

Because the Quality Director has to have the authority and support of the CEO, the most logical person to supervise the Quality Director is the CEO. If not, the Quality Director will be defeated by the system, i.e., the four barriers to quality.

#76 *You cannot inspect quality into the product; you have to build quality into the process and system.*

GANGSTER

Story #77

At a company picnic, I noticed that 10% to 20% of the employees have cute children. They tried to make them even more cute by dressing them in gangster attire—the baggy pants and those things that signify gangs. Yes, the children looked cute, but what were these parents thinking about?

This is one thing that came out in the classes we have—how we perceive one another. I have found while working in sales, the first five seconds after someone meets you is the most important time for you. During that brief period, the person makes a subconscious decision about you and who you are. During the class, I emphasize that we should not do anything to defeat ourselves.

Even though we dress our children like gang-bangers, they may not be gang-bangers; they may be some of the best kids in the world, but what do people think? The people in your community are going to come to a conclusion about them because of how they look. This means your child already has a strike against him because of a false perception. There was a study where the researchers took six people and dressed three as prisoners and three as guards. The six were not told the nature of the experiment. Within two days they started acting out the roles for which they were dressed. The three prisoners acted aggressively and loud, disapproving of everything; the three guards were assertive, in charge and cold. My position is this. If our children are dressed like gangster, not only are they going to be perceived by others as gang-bangers, but they may believe and act like gang-bangers. In class we talked about what we are doing to our children. Many of our employees didn't have any idea of how they were programming their children. There has to be an awareness and knowledge to help our employees.

One of the big arguments was, "They should like me for who I am." That's fine, but whether we like it or not, we make our own prejudiced perceptions based on our past experiences and environment.

Let's say there are two teachers walking toward you. One looks like a burned out hippie and the other looks like a business professional with a briefcase. Who would you give your child to for training and teaching? Even though you may want to talk with them and find out who they are, you may not be given that opportunity. If you had to make the decision based on appearance, who would you choose? Everybody I asked that question voted, obviously, for the clean-cut guy because they felt he was more educated, that he cared more about his job, and that he appeared to be in a position of authority and represented it well.

As the employees looked at this, the light came on as to how they or their children were perceived. This awareness is very important in how we raise our children. It can be either positive or negative. The class taught the employees that we have more influence on our children than we think we do.

Another example we use is the parent who takes his child to a parent/teacher conference and the father sits with arms crossed and dressed in a gang-banger fashion, glaring at the teacher. Put yourself in that teacher's position. Regardless of how well she does in teaching and training that child, if she doesn't get support from the home and parents, it will be much less effective.

At some time, she will make a subconscious decision whether or not to help your child. Teachers are too underpaid and understaffed to try to personally touch each child; consequently, she will make a decision about the child.

As you can see, personal presentation is very important. Another example might be the employee applying for a bank loan. What if he dresses in a sloppy fashion wearing sunglasses? Do you think the loan officer is going to readily loan money to him? Don't do anything to defeat yourself.

#77 *We are who we perceive ourselves to be.*

SHUT-DOWN EMPLOYEE

Story #78

A profile of a shut-down employee is one who comes into the program and sits at the back of the class or in the corner, with his arms crossed and slouched in the chair, looking like he wants to whip the world. The numbers indicate consistently that 99% of the employees are good employees and 1% are bad employees. Five percent will not jump on board right away, but 4% percent eventually come around. This 5% are usually the shut-down employees.

They have probably been with the company for a while. This employee may have come to the company with the attitude that they were going to excel by working extra hard doing their job. But as time went on, the lack of systems beats the employee into submission. Other causes may have been a negative co-worker, managers, hidden agendas, double standards, or the four barriers to quality.

It usually takes 9 to 18 months for the employee to shut-down. He has seen many programs come and go and his philosophy is that the company will never change. He tried to do things the company asked him to do, but all they've done is suck the wind and energy out of his sails. His attitude is stale to my program at the onset.

Usually the term shut-down employee and bad employee are synonymous in the company. These employees are simply frustrated and just want to do their job and be left alone. When conflict and chaos start, they are either very short-tempered or just don't want to hear about it. They typically are cold to other employees because they have had enough and avoidance is their defense mechanism.

Usually shut-down employees can end up being some of your best employees and team members. It's rewarding to watch them as you move through the program. It usually takes them about 12 to 18 months to come around. These are the people we want to help grow in the organization because of their knowledge, expertise and work ethics.

> #78 *A shut- down employee with potential is the biggest waste within an organization.*

WORKING THROUGH NEGATIVE RAP

Story #79

There's something in some people's personality that only allows them to communicate with another person in a negative way. For example, you walk up to someone and your first comment is, "Hey, man, it looks like you just woke up on the wrong side of the bed today." He may come back and say, "Well, at least I'm not driving that piece of junk to work every day like you do." You respond, "Well, at least I'm not living with an ugly wife." This type of conversation can go on and on. Soon it carries over into everything. We're totally naive and untruthful to ourselves if we think we can turn it off and on whenever we want.

It's hard not to communicate the same way with our customers, when this is how we talk day to day with other employees. When we're sitting and dealing with customers or fellow employees, they might smile and laugh. We have employees tell us they've been friends for 25 years and they've always done that. What happens when someone has a bad night and comes to work in a bad mood? He's not going to want to listen to a bunch of negative rap. When it starts, a confrontation ensues.

Emotions are always moving up and down. If we are engaging in negative rap, all it does is lead to negativism. It's like a cancer and will eat away at a company; before you know it, you're taking it home and it's creating problems there too. As you sit around the breakfast table in the morning, be conscious of how many negative things you say to your children. Stand up straight, don't eat your cereal so fast, chew with your mouth closed. We're programming ourselves and our children in this kind of negative environment.

The mind can't separate what's play and what's not. If some guy says, "Hey Bruce, you're ugly," I might laugh and put it off. In reality though, it registers as a negative rap and will eventually build up. Eventually, I might explode; then we've got chaos on our hands.

Negative rap leads to no good. It's one of the things we really need to get out of a company. When we are negative about everything, no matter what we put on the table—it's going to be negative. If we're not careful, people will start shutting down because of the attitudes. Negative rap is very bad for any organization.

> #79 *Let's become aware of how we communicate with one another and focus on the positive side of life.*

FLAVOR OF THE MONTH

Story #80

The "Flavor of the Month" is what's hot for that particular company in a given month. We're going to do "quality" this month. Everybody heads in that direction for a time, as they define quality. Next month it might be "communication". And the following month might be a series of meetings on a particular train of thought or philosophy in sales. This goes on and on and promotes distrust in a company. Watch out for getting into the "Flavor of the Month." Stick with the basics. Your first question should be, "How are you going to make it happen?" "How will that happen on the job." Look at the "Flavor of the Month" and question that person as to how can you make it work within your organization. Believe me, it's not going to happen without BaseWork Centers, consistency and accountability. With the "Flavor of the Month," you throw away hard-earned training dollars. The company must support its training department and encourage it to develop a long-term training program and stick with it.

> #80 *Look out for new packaging of old concepts with no substance.*

REINFORCEMENT DAILY

Story #81

I was sitting in a marketing class at University of Southern California taught by Nick Anderson. The lecture concerned basic 100-level marketing ideas. This should not have been new information for me; after all, my college major was marketing and business management. As I listened, it occurred to me that here were some basic marketing ideas that I had forgotten. The lecture discussed things I was currently doing in business and reinforced everything I was doing in my program.

What does reinforcement have to do with business? People battle insecurity in their organization on a daily basis. Consequently, they need daily reinforcement concerning appropriate business values. My program teaches those values through the four barriers to quality, the BaseWork Center concept, brainstorming, problem-solving, doing the right thing and caring for one another. Because we can't always remember these things, they must continually be reinforced in our work place.

Let's take a look at advertising. If all the pizza industry had to do to convince people to buy their product was advertise pizza one time, we would only see one commercial. But how many commercials do we see for pizza? They are constantly reinforcing the idea in our heads so we will, in fact, buy pizza over other food.

If you look at a quality program in an office and you are trained on it once and see one or two memos about it, pretty soon it falls by the wayside. We'd be smart to remember the advertising principle and apply it to the office situation by constantly reinforcing quality issues—our rules, our beliefs and our feelings. We'd also keep a direct line of communication open to every employee in the organization via the team meetings.

My meeting at the University of Southern California was a good reminder to me of the importance of daily reinforcement in keeping things fresh—otherwise they may be dismissed or forgotten. There's also a related use for reinforcement. It applies to our children. We must constantly reinforce the positive—love, commitment, guidance.

> #81 *To have a continuously improving organization, the value and basis of the quality program must be reinforced daily.*

MIKE SMITH

Story #82

Mike is an excellent example of someone growing up in a family business. Over the years, his perspective changed as he viewed the business from different management vantage points. One day he emerged as President of a very large company with many employees, finding himself doing things to which he was unaccustomed. As a company grows the four barriers to quality start to show up along with the family's lack of basic management skills in running the business. Remember, when he first started, it was just the owner and maybe one other employee. Then as the business grows, the entrepreneur, out of an established habit, tries to continue running the entire business.

The owner can manage it when it's small, but as it grows and becomes a larger business with many employees, he has to start formalizing business. Processes and systems begin to take shape and assume more importance. The business is now too large for the entrepreneur to manage everything; he has to start delegating, and the only way to do that is to formalize the way business is conducted (build business infrastructures).

Another of the typical things that happen as the business grows, is that a great deal of inefficiency starts leaking into the company. The typical response, because cash flow is usually high by this time, is to throw money and bodies at the problem. That is okay unless sales peak, level, or drop and the cash flow slows down. The owner then has a tough time servicing the inefficiencies and the corporate debts that have grown with the business.

The biggest challenge, then, of growing businesses is to formalize the way they're doing business regarding family members and new employees. Depending on how well the formalization occurs, the company will either become stagnant, die on the vine, or grow. It's a tough situation for the entrepreneur who has made the company grow; he must now start to let go. When the inefficiencies show up, the owner has to do something. The first thing most of them do is cut expenses (usually payroll), as opposed to looking for ways to improve. When we cut payroll without regard for who does what, real problems can result.

Mike Smith is totally responsible for my starting BaseWork Systems 2000, because of his undying trust and commitment and the desire to do what was right and fair. In the beginning, we went through some tough times but survived. Mike learned; I learned. We now step back and can hardly believe the challenge we took on. Initially, we didn't even have a formal way of approaching the change. Mike not only trusted me, but had an undying loyalty to the program, which I appreciated so much. He gave me the support and confidence to continue.

Letting go is the toughest thing an entrepreneur or businessman can do, removing the ego and stepping back allowing a program to work. He must allow the process to happen and allow his way of doing business to be formalized.

> #82 *The key to success is delegating to a formal, well-trained, and defined organization and having the trust in your organization to let go.*

EMPLOYEES AS FREE AGENTS

Story #83

Do you know what is happening right now, right here in Orange County California and across the nation in 1997? Many, many businesses are scrambling to get good employees, and guess what? There is no real shortage of these talented job seekers. Even with the seemingly large number of qualified applicants, these potential employees are exercising quite a bit of negotiating strength.

The first question I ask myself is, "Why are these people not working?" The answer is simple: they have either been humiliated, disgraced, poked fun at, laid off, down-sized, out-sourced to death, or they have barely been surviving financially over the last three to four years. The unemployment or under-employment was a result of the re-engineering of our economy where payrolls were reduced and jobs eliminated. Now, all of a sudden, we seem to be getting healthy again—or could it be that business deduced that it had screwed up? Regardless, there are now qualified people in the labor force looking at numerous openings. Could it be that they are in the driver's seat?

A quality company is going to look at not only how it can retain its employees, but also how it can grow the employees. I have seen companies go out and try to buy a salesman, maybe a star on a community sports team. The star has no loyalty to the company at all, which may result in under performance. If allowed to continue, that sets up a double standard hurting the employees that have been there and have been paying the price. For a company to develop a loyal employee base, it needs to treat the employees with respect while addressing the four barriers to quality. Companies should grow employees internally and promote from within.

Many in management question the role of training when it appears that, once trained, the employee moves on and goes to a competitor. My question is, "If we are training them and they're leaving, why?" More than likely we didn't see their value and they felt unhappy, or maybe they were being held down by someone within the company. Most talented people will go out and seek other opportunity if unhappy.

The best thing for us to do is to grow an informed, happy workforce. We do this through long-term commitment, through training, and through encouragement. If the employees are to continually improve and grow mentally and emotionally with the company and in their home lives and in the community, the company must take responsibility.

There are many companies out there that went through tough times. The strong entrepreneur simply persevered. When times were tough and the easiest thing to do was to cut payroll, he held on to his employees and searched for ways to allow them to hang on.

Now, with the economy turning upward, these are the people that are leading the industry; and it's because of their employee base. They are able to move and grow a lot faster than their competition because they have created a good base of loyalty and commitment from their employees. It goes back to BaseValues: 1) do what is morally and ethically correct, and 2) treat everybody as you want to be treated. You do that and you reap the benefits. In the long term, it will come back to you and your company.

Don't get caught in the belief that you should not train your employees because they'll go somewhere else, or that training is expensive. Yes, it may be expensive, that's true; we simply need to budget for it. Believe me, if we don't train, all the inefficiencies will kill the business. The statistics show that for every one dollar spent on training there is a 30 dollar return. That's a pretty strong statistic.

> #83 *Your employee loyalty is not built overnight, and it can't be bought— it has to be earned.*

JUSTIFY

Story #84

To justify is to defend. Justifying typically occurs as part of the negotiation process or in relation to the way we are doing business. An employee can usually justify the means by referencing the end.

If employees feel they are being attacked, they will shift into their justification mode regarding the specific issue. When justification clicks in, reality has a tendency to click out.

The reason a lot of us get into this trap internally is because we are being attacked and don't know what else to do. It would be more productive if we had a process for problem-solving or for expressing our thoughts and actions in regard to the quality issues in question.

Companies need to work on systems that, instead of putting employees into personal jousting matches, provide them a mechanism for sitting down and looking at the issues. This is typically done by removing the fear in the organization and assaulting the other barriers to quality. If an employee feels he is not going to get reprimanded for his action, then he will be more apt to sit down and discuss the issue and how to resolve it.

We have to become better at removing the personal feelings from negotiations and moving more toward resolving issues. To get involved in an argument, point fingers, and try to place blame only makes a person defensive. Remember, people who fortify their defenses can't and won't move. That's why many situations become hostile.

#84 *Forget blame—focus on the solution and move on.*

JUST ASK

Story #85

If you want help solving a problem, opening up communication, or getting people involved, put employees in a situation where they can ask and/or respond to questions. If a company or employee has a problem, one of the best things to do is simply ask for help. Asking for help or input is not a sign of weakness; actually it displays a position of strength. It projects that you have strength enough in your character to ask for help. If you'll notice people that are insecure and have a lot of problems both at home and at work, usually they have a tough time asking for help or information. If a company wants to look at its problems and try to solve them, the easiest and most efficient route is to ask the employees, especially those who have to live with the problems on a daily basis. Oftentimes, they have known the answer for some time; it's just that no one ever asked.

Don't let the "asking for help is a weakness" mentality become a part of your culture. It is a great asset and even a skill when people can talk and communicate at work and at home. A lot of information is out there, yet goes unaccessed because our insecurities or the environment of the organization doesn't allow us to ask questions. If we are shut-down at work and don't ask questions, we're probably doing the same at home. It's an unhealthy and unproductive attitude in either place.

#85 *It takes greater strength internally to accept help than to give help when asked.*

LOSING THE PERSONALITY
OF THE FOUNDER

Story #86

Visualize this scenario! You have a company where the entrepreneur is of unquestionable integrity and is probably one of the finest people I have ever met. He is sincere and really tries to do what is right. His problem is that his company grew past his capacity to manage it. The sales moved along for eight years and all of a sudden, at nine years, he was doing $10 million. If you haven't guessed by now, the entrepreneur's background is in sales.

As sales increased, he had to become more involved in manufacturing. He ended up in the plant running the manufacturing because he had established a good client base. Even as he spent more time in manufacturing, sales continued growing. All of a sudden, this strong entrepreneur felt he needed some accounting help.

In came a CFO who took away all the headaches of the entrepreneur, including the managing of the day-to-day business and all the number-crunching. The CFO proved to be a blessing for the entrepreneur. Almost with a sigh of relief, the entrepreneur gave the CFO free reign to do pretty much what he wanted.

As the years crept by and the CFO got more power, the entrepreneur began to understand less and less about **his** company and the running of it. Management was actually not what he believed it to be.

Indirectly, this is what I believe was an internal power play. The CFO ended up running the company, even though the entrepreneur was still the boss and President of the organization. Based on his training, the CFO had a tendency to run the business by numbers alone, possessing the good business sense to know that you can't spend more than you take in. He realized that in order to stay in business, you must make money with expenses not exceeding revenue.

As the lack of systems and inefficiencies started to grow and as sales flattened out, the company no longer had the cash flow to support the inefficiencies. The CFO then started examining the numbers, the only thing he really understood. It then became a classic example of not improving business but just cutting payroll. In cutting payroll, he still wasn't getting the necessary expenses down and soon discovered that the company couldn't get the product out, thus it made no money. Quarter by quarter the company felt they needed to cut payroll, instead of looking back to the long-term plans for ways to formalize the way business was conducted. The formalization of process and building business infrastructure should have started day one with the company. The longer you wait, the tougher it becomes to build business infrastructure because you are building bad habits that may prove hard to break.

The CFO had some insecurity and possibly some hidden agendas that ultimately made it difficult to represent the best interest of the founder and of the organization. Soon, it came into question how he was treating people and what he felt was of value in regard to personal integrity.

As the company grows and develops, it is important for the CEO to run the business and still be involved; he can't hand it off. The job of the CFO is to train and teach the entrepreneur and the company how to conduct business. The numbers and resulting data analysis are very important and provide an accurate barometer of what is happening within the company. Later, because the company was lacking cash, it went out and raised money, then bought a couple other companies, but ultimately ended up not able to manage itself. They outgrew their capacity all across the board. It was not just accounting or management, but also included manufacturing and every department.

The toughest decision for the company now was deciding where to start to solve the problems. Obviously, it was the perfect time to implement the BaseWork Systems, and thus gain the direction and the tools necessary to move from an informal to a formal way of doing business.

In this company we had to play politics because of the Board's and the original owner's involvement in the transition process. It was a huge case of egos, insecurities, and lack of trust across the spectrum.

My hat is off to this company! For whatever reason, they recognized the need to make some changes and move on. They realized they had to move from a quarter to quarter mentality, to a long-term perspective.

> #86 *There is nothing more damaging to an organization and to a relationship than an employee of power with hidden agendas.*

EMPLOYEES WELCOME ACOUNTABILITY

Story #87

One of the things I hear from management is that employees don't want to be held accountable. That's simply not true! My position is that if we haven't defined the way we are doing business, how can we hold anyone accountable? That is even truer if employees have not been trained—and guess what? You can't have proper training until you've defined the jobs and BaseWork Centers and lock them together into correct processes and systems.

A philosophy of business contends that we have management to hold our employees accountable. My program will cause a dramatic change in that philosophy! The employees will start to hold each other accountable because they want to hold each other accountable. We talked earlier about employees who don't like being held accountable. Remember, they fall into the one percent that has learned to manipulate the lack of systems and processes. The other 99 percent of your employees welcome accountability because they have always been accountable. The frustrating thing before was that accountability in an informal organization was consistently a moving target, fueled by the four barriers to quality. The thing they desire most is that *everyone* be held accountable. Once employees agree on what they're going to do, *all* employees and managers will/must be held accountable.

#87 Only 1% of your organization does not welcome accountability.

CHURNING MANAGEMENT

Story #88

A lot of companies have gotten into what I call *churning management*, where the manager is there for short-term goals— maybe two to three years. Their goal may be to cut the cost of doing business by 15% over a two-year period. Out of that 15%, they may get a one or two percent bonus.

Unfortunately, I have seen this time and time again. The churching of upper, lower, and middle management is short-term management strategy at its worst, causing the manager to hit his numbers at any expense. Remember, we've talked about this; instead of improving the way they're doing business (long term), they just cut expenses (usually payroll) short term.

I have seen employees cut and the remainder step up and take on the slack for sixteen to eighteen months until they finally burn out or shut-down. In the interim, the manager, who cut the expenses and got his bonus, is gone to another company to start the same process again.

If churning management is an ongoing procedure, how long is American business going to be able to stay in business? The answer is, "Not long!" Not unless they start beefing up again. If they do that, the cycle is likely to repeat itself. Look what's happening: we are tearing down, building up, and running our employees ragged.

Churning managers is not good. If the CEO/President approaches business with a long-term vision and commitment to the organization and goals that ensure employees a good income and steady jobs, then the company will continue to make a profit.

> *#88* *Lets start a new fad that pays incentive bonuses for keeping employees, growing the business, and improving the process.*

AN INTERVIEW WITH TOM VAUGHN

Story #89

I'm including this interview so you can hear first-hand what others think about my approach to quality.

Please excuse any grammatical inconsistencies that might be included. To ensure accuracy, I had the interviews transcribed exactly as recorded. You know how it is when you're talking, sometimes your tongue gets wrapped around your eye tooth and you can't see what you're saying. In other words, please excuse any errors that offend the English teacher in you.

Bruce: "You've been with your company 22 years and retired. Tom, what do you feel overall about our positions on the four barriers to quality: fear, communication, training and procedure?"

Tom: "I don't think there is any question at all that **fear** is the biggest obstacle for any company. I noticed as the program developed, that a lot of the fellows that were laborers or workers and had very little to say about anything, when they were given the privilege to express themselves without worrying about being in trouble or losing their job, or being punished in some way, great ideas came from them. It unleashes a mental capacity that is there, and we don't know about it until we remove the fear and allow people to express themselves and talk abut it. I believe your program does that."

Bruce: "Many companies and programs never address our two rules: 1) do what is morally and ethically correct, and 2) treat everybody as you want to be treated, and when it's in conflict it's a quality issue. Tell us what you think about that and how it might have helped, and what you think personally about a company having these two rules."

Tom: "I think those are two rules that everybody grew up with in the back of their minds. They are heartfelt rules that everyone wants to see. If the worst of people want to see it and expect it, they'll point it out in someone quicker than anything—they're unfair or can't be trusted. I think that as long as those two rules prevail, people have the freedom to go on and express themselves and take part in that kind of attitude. If that's not present, then you have a division among people. It keeps them from having the freedom to express themselves and say what is on their mind for fear of being put down and shut down. So, until we can be ethically and morally straight with our people and ourselves and our neighbor, we won't get the best of them."

Bruce: "Do you think the program helped the communication, making the people feel a little more a part—not just management but the factory workers and the floor operations?"

Tom: "There is no question that the program offered them that opportunity and there were consistently regular meetings that they had the privilege of speaking up at. In the meeting, they were expected to express themselves. All people have good ideas and basically have good morals and wish to express those but need the freedom to do so."

Bruce: "Tom, you've been around other companies. What did you think at the start of the program? We talk about in the book that there hasn't been much consistency in most programs. They start and stop. We've tried different programs and slogans. What did you think when we first started and what were your thoughts when we started talking about a quality program?"

Tom: "When the program first started, I knew that we needed something because I was in middle management and worked very closely with upper management and was in many of the meetings. I could see the gap between the upper management and the workers. I could see there wasn't the respect needed to allow people to have the freedom to express themselves and to take advantage of the knowledge that was there from all the employees. I knew if they were given the freedom to express themselves, it would increase the quality of everything. Once you give people the opportunity to express themselves and be a part of the program and let them contribute, the quality will increase because they are 'buying in' so to speak, of the business. That instills pride and quality control and increases the quality of their work. And this allows for constructive criticism in what they're doing and it will cause them to want to do better."

Bruce: "Tom, we've talked about departmental walls, between upper and lower management, between the employees and management, and management and unions. Do you feel these things exist in companies?"

Tom: "I think anytime you have two different departments they automatically exist because first of all when something goes wrong, one department is not going to want to take responsibility of what another department did. This creates what I call a negative atmosphere. Rather than everyone pulling together for the end results, they'll then say this is what I'm supposed to do and I don't really care. This happens when you allow walls to be built between departments. **Barriers** is an even better word because it stops progress from one department to the other. One person stops when he gets what he needs to done, rather than breaking those barriers down and caring about the other person and being concerned about what the end result will be."

Bruce: "We've talked about a frustrated, shut-down employee. Can you identify with that statement? Not necessarily yourself but with other employees as far as how we say that employees really want to do a good job but the lack of systems kicks the energy out of them and then they go to what we call shut down. What are your thoughts on that?"

Tom: "I think that is a very present condition in many companies—especially larger companies. I have seen it where I have worked. For example, we had a young fellow that was productive in our department. He was in lower management but took pride in his work. But he was under continued scrutiny from his superior. That went on for several years until the fellow had an opportunity to transfer out of that department and go into something else. When he did that, even though he was under heavy scrutiny, the department he left went down. It could not produce as it had under his leadership. He was shut down. No matter what he said or what he offered, it was never right or good enough, and finally he just wouldn't offer anything. And the opportunity came and he transferred out and left a big hole. So this is true in any company."

Bruce: "And, Tom, when we talk about shut down and the guy just sits back and nods his head and agrees, would you agree with that statement?"

Tom: "Yes I do agree with that. I also think it goes farther than that. They'll get so shut down that they won't even nod and agree. They'll just sit there."

Bruce: "Tom, we've talked in the program about creating a balance in your life between your home life and work life. Our position in the program is we have never seen a guy that can be good at work and bad at home, or bad at work and good at home. Or something at work does not affect home, or visa versa. Would you agree with that statement?"

Tom: "I totally agree that in general that is true. Especially when things are not right at home. That is a very important part of a man's life and it will affect him at work. It is also true that unnecessarily bad situations at work are hard for a man to leave at work and so he takes it home and then it begins to affect his home life. A man is at work most of his waking hours in a day and until the atmosphere at work can be created where he can be content and happy in what he is doing, several things are not going to happen. First of all, he won't have quality at work, and he won't have a quality home life like he should have."

Bruce: "We've talked also about caring for one another and helping each other through the tough things at work. The old cliche we've all heard is "leave your problems at home. Don't bring them to work." Tom, how many people do you know that can leave them at home and not affect them at work? We say a lot of people need someone to talk to, and because we're at work most of the time there is really no one else to talk to. Especially if the situation at home is not good."

Tom: "If their situation at home is not a good environment, I think you've touched on the very center nerve of man because, first of all, home and the home life of man was created long before the job was created. And when a man's very core part of his life is affected, then you've affected his total life and I don't think it's wise to expect or to tell him to leave his problems at home. He can't do it. It's not possible. He's not created that way."

Bruce: "Tom, have you seen these guys that explode at work because problems just build up and get to a point where they're a walking time bomb. I don't necessarily mean physical violence. Do you see where we talk about having no way to vent problems, hostilities, troubles, or concerns that it can build up into something if we don't have an avenue of release?"

Tom: "Well, that's certainly true. We've heard recently of companies where they have had people come into their companies and actually kill someone. And so, they have not had the opportunity of venting and they finally blow up. That is usually over a long period of time before someone will do that. When that's happening I wonder how much damage that has created to the productivity of that person, or perhaps what it's done to the quality control of the product they are manufacturing. I think until a company can develop an avenue for the people to express themselves without being condemned or fear their losing their job, you won't see their full potential. It certainly won't do them any good in their home lives."

Bruce: "And, then so the basis of the program being the Four Barriers to Quality, we feel it is just as important internally—our head and our heart—to talk and communicate as it is to perform that procedure, job, or training. Tom, you've seen other programs. Do you feel the four barriers to quality is a step in the right direction?

Tom:"I think it has to be the beginning of accomplishing anything in helping man to overcome some of the negatives that keep him from becoming a productive person that he really desires to be. I think that he is a living being. He's first physical, has flesh—but he also has a soul and a spirit. All three of those must function with the freedom to express themselves and be content. If that doesn't happen and you shut that person down in some part of his life, he is not going to be that productive person or the happy person that creates contentment for the people he works with and around which must happen. This must be something that is generated amongst all people in a company so they can have the freedom to express themselves and accomplish what they want to."

Bruce: "Tom, we've talked about the four barriers to quality, walking the walk, and talking the talk, and our two rules. Do you feel that the Bruce Snell Group lived up to their rules?"

Tom: "Yes. I believe that there has been a consistency there that has certainly caught my eye as I went through two years with the Bruce Snell Group. I was amazed at times at some of the difficulties that could have taken control of the program and how well they were cared for. The consistency of saying this is what happened, but this is what could happen if we do certain things that were pointed out. And I saw many of those things worked out. I now think that is one of the important factors in the Bruce Snell program. If people are allowed to be consistent with quality, with moral and ethical issues and allowed to practice that, and are reminded to practice that and keep it in front of them, then the Bruce Snell program will be effective in any company.

Bruce: Tom, since you've been in several different work environments, do you feel that any one of these functions can carry a program focusing just on fear and not communication, not on procedure or training? Or maybe just do training and not work on the other things. We put these four barriers together after six or seven years. Do you agree that there is no short cut—you can't pick it apart?"

Tom: "I don't think you can separate them because they all have to come together and be appreciated by all involved for the program to be all that the Bruce Snell Group expects it to be, and all that any company expects it to be. I think it's the worst thing that can happen to anybody. Whether it is in a company, home life, sporting event or whatever. Fear cripples. And until we break the fear or the control of fear, then we really sort of get in our shell and stay there."

Bruce: "Now, Tom, would you recommend the program to another company?"

Tom: "Without question."

Bruce: "Then our next question is after your retirement, you are buying stock in the Bruce Snell Group. Why?"

Tom: "I have been in industry for a lot of years and I have seen the things that are out there and have experienced them myself. I believe that the Bruce Snell Program has something to offer. I believe what it is doing is taking some age-old things that have always been there and bringing them together in a program that will work; that will give individuals the freedom to not only express themselves, but accomplish things they would like to accomplish as individuals. And when you have that, then I can't see how any company can't progress and become what they set out to become. So, I want to invest in the Bruce Snell Group because not only the world needs to rethink how they're doing business, why they're doing business, and what they are really trying to accomplish."

Bruce: Tom, do you think other people feel the same way you do as far as not just in your company but out in the market, dealing with other suppliers or other companies? You think other people share your views?"

Tom: "Bruce, I have had the privilege of talking to people all over this nation and in some foreign countries and I hear the same story regardless of where I go. Companies are not caring for their employees. They're more interested in the bottom line—whatever they have to do to get there. Maybe it's because they have stockholders or whatever. But the word is still out there amongst the working people that they're not cared for any more. There is nothing more degrading to man than to think he is doing something and think he's not being appreciated or cared for. I think that if a company and its top management will take the Bruce Snell program and use it the way it is written and taught, it will enhance them in every way."

Bruce: "Now, you brought up a good point. We talk about written commitments from the top management and how important it is for them to talk the talk and walk the walk. Do you feel as strongly as we do that it's not going to happen without top management's support?"

Tom: "I don't think it can happen until you can establish a program that everyone knows what the agenda is for each department from top management down. Every department that is affected by top management, which should be every one of them, can believe that they really care and have adopted the program. Then it will be a long, slow process for even middle management to make this happen even though they might want it very badly. Until they believe that top management has bought into the program and believes in it—it won't happen."

Bruce: "Tom, we say that it takes about two years for the change and the consistency. And, again, you've been in programs that promise the world that in a quarter, a month or a few weeks they can accomplish x, y, and z. What do you feel about the two years, as far as taking that time to change or improve that organization?"

Tom: "Well, I don't think you can do anything in a company of any size in less than two years. First of all, I think it takes close to a year to find out where a company is at, what they really need, and then how to make the program wrap around them and fit all the different problems they may have and fit the organization. It takes two years for everybody to buy into it. It takes time for any company, meaning employees, to look at a program, test it, try it, prove it, that it's real and it works and it can help. There will be some employees that will grab it and run with it, and that's a real plus. But then there are those who stand out on the fringes and watch what happens and say, 'I've got to see it; it sounds too good to be true.' There's an old cliche that if it sounds too good to be true, it probably is. But I believe the program is good and has a lot to offer to individuals, to departments, to the company. I certainly support it."

Bruce: "We'll end on this question, Tom. Your plant had a lot of Spanish employees and they were great supporters of the program. You also had a lot of employees coming back and saying that they had learned skills to help at home in regards to communicating with their wife and children. What are your thoughts on that?"

Tom: "Well, it's probably the first program that I've been around that would take the Spanish speaking people or those of any other language for that matter and stay with them helping them to deal with some of the things they go through. We have barriers ourselves in American companies that we struggle with, but when you have a language barrier too, it becomes a compound fracture, if you will. These people are continually struggling with this language barrier as well as try to contend with emotional and mental problems that come up in organizations. I think that was one of the great marks of this program. That it stays with people regardless of where they're at. You really can't help anyone until you meet them where they're at. Until you can identify with them and where they're at, and what they're problems might be, you really don't know how to help them."

Bruce: "Could you see personal growth in these people?"

Tom: "I've seen a lot of personal growth in people. And I believe the program can help people at home. One of the biggest problems in any home is communication and it's a problem across the board. Until people can communicate in a way that they will hear each other and listen to what is being said, you have a real problem. So many people in their homes don't know how to talk to each other. They do a lot of talking and that could be considered communication. But communicating is when you've said something, and someone heard it. And then they feel the freedom to use it in their life. That is how life will change and how homes become better places to live, because of a program like this."

Bruce: "Well, Tom we appreciate your time. Is there anything you would like to end with?"

Tom: "Just to share that I think it's a great program. One that the world needs—this nation needs. I encourage anyone who has an opportunity to give it a good try."

Bruce: "Thanks, Tom."

13
LIFE'S LESSONS

This chapter is a compilation of Life's Lessons from various stories that I have written. Because so many people comment on the lessons, I decided to fill a chapter with them. Read and enjoy—each is a lesson learned in the MBA of life.

1. When dealing with tough decisions, deal only with data and not emotion.
2. The focus of addressing a quality issue is not in pinning the blame, but in coming to an solution.
3. The two rules are: 1) do what is morally and ethically correct, and 2) treat everybody as you want to be treated.
4. Corporate needs to move from a dictatorial "do as I say" attitude to a more "how can I help you do your job" attitude. Corporate's main job should be to help its employees, divisions and companies do a better job.
5. Sometimes the simplest thing to your customer is the most frustrating thing.
6. A procedure is only good when it is held accountable. Everyone in the organization should understand break-even analysis and the cost of doing business in their particular BaseWork Center. Only then can we make informed decisions based on data.

7. Be aware of the carrier of hidden agendas. His fertile ground is usually around the coffee pot or water fountain and is always informal.

8. "What-ifing" the deal to death is a danger and a perilous disease for an organization.

9. Double standards are the quickest way to deflate a company's morale.

10. What is good for the goose is sometimes hard to swallow for the gander.

11. Do not buy any product or service that does not define its training by the company's BaseWork Centers or jobs.

12. Do not look at the training budget as an expense, but as an investment and an asset of your company.

13. The best people to help you design what is needed for training internally within your organization are your employees and that person doing the particular task.

14. The only way change is going to happen in an organization is for an employee to feel secure in that organization.

15. The path of change is taken a step at a time and measured in miles and months.

16. Short-term winners at the expense of another usually end up long term-losers.

17. You cannot define jobs and BaseWork Centers, systems, or processes until you come to an agreement on the actual corporate structure. Research typically reveals that corporate structure differs from perception to reality.

18. The gloves of quality and change are worn by the hands of integrity and trust.

19. Beware of the manager who says, "I am just so busy I can't afford to plan or schedule my day; I don't have time."

20. To try to create a multiple location quality program is unrealistic without the development of a corporate model.

21. Interpersonal skill awareness brings new life to an organization and the community.

22. Our organizations will become the universities of tomorrow with the employees being the students.
23. A lesson learned from a negative experience is positive.
24. Frustration is knowing the solution to the problem, yet not possessing the responsibility nor trust to resolve it.
25. In an informal organization, the job priority is the priority of the day.
26. Stay away from the negative person because he will suck the life, breath and enthusiasm out of you and your organization.
27. An organization has to be socially responsible to its employees, community and country in both its short- and long-term thinking. If a company is socially responsible and committed to its employees, then it will meet the needs of the community and the country.
28. No system is too complex when the people doing the actual job take it apart process by process, step by step and procedure by procedure.
29. If an employee is to have a manual about his BaseWork Center with accurate processes, steps, procedures and additional duties, the manual needs to be written by the employee.
30. To make decisions based on data, we must qualify the data, manage, and monitor the data. If we are not managing and monitoring the data collected, then why do we need to collect it?
31. Sitting on the sideline is comfortable if you are a spectator; however, building a quality company is not a spectator sport.
32. Some of the brightest talent in your organization has not yet begun to turn on their lights.
33. When addressing employee conflict, remove your and the company's emotions from the deal, and deal only with facts and data.
34. Beware of a new name for an old problem.

35. Total Quality Management must be placed in the hands of the employees with leadership from a totally committed management.

36. Taking one step away from logical thinking and common sense is a step in the wrong direction.

37. The best time to build business infrastructure is at the business conception and start. The best time is before you don't have time.

38. You can't have quality before you have a base foundation of doing what is morally and ethically correct, treating everybody as you want to be treated, and holding everybody accountable for that treatment.

39. We must move the quick fix, quick action, putting out the fire, instant gratification mentality to a long-term process of system improvement. Instead of jumping to the quick fix or quick solution, we need to ask why that problem is happening.

40. The open door policy in most organizations is shut.

41. The life of an organization is the development and training of its greatest assets—its employees.

42. The most undervalued asset in an organization is its employees and their potential.

43. An employee's quality of work is in direct correlation with their quality of mental and emotional well-being.

44. Line-item management hardly ever provides long-term solutions for the improvement of the way we are doing business.

45. The program has found that 99% of employees in an organization are good employees. As the employees move through the program, we find that 5% of the employee base resist the program for a variety of reasons. Statistically, 4% of that 5% get on board the program usually between months eighteen and twenty-four leaving 1% of the employee base. Again statistically 1% of employees are bad employees and

they will remove themselves from the program and more than likely from the company.

46. 99% the employees in an organization are good employees and accept and encourage accountability.

47. 1% of the employees in an organization are bad employees that eat away at the integrity of that organization. Don't make rules directed at that 1% that affect the other 99% negatively, deal with the problem created by the 1%.

48. When resolving issues, don't spend energy in a negative fashion by trying to justify or pin blame for that particular problem; spend that energy focusing on how to resolve the issue.

49. In order for an organization to become a quality organization, the owner/CEO/President has to have total support and buy off from his board as well as the share holders. In doing this, he must move from short-term thinking to long-term planning and direction. The CEO must lead this transformation via available tools designed to manage and monitor the process through accurate data.

50. Even though the sky of an organization is full of stars, they will never shine without the commitment and direction of leadership.

51. There is never the right or opportune time for an organization to start the implementation of a quality program—just start.

52. Growth without formalizing the way we do business, is a sure fire way to lose the personality of the founder of the organization.

53. With training, direction, and the right tools, most children of the founders can lead that organization into the next generation.

54. A quality organization moves from management holding employees accountable for quality to employees being responsible and personally accountable. They in fact don't pass on or accept non-quality. This means that, in effect, employees are now holding one another accountable for

quality in every process, step, procedure and system in that organization.

55. Departmentally, quotas and incentives usually build departmental walls which become barriers to quality. They do this by creating competition from one department to the other, resulting in one department winning and another losing. The ultimate loser is going to be the customer as well as the company's long-term client base.

56. A positive company attitude is contagious and attracts customers.

57. A good positive attitude in the morning sets the tone for a good positive work day.

58. Take daily accounts of your wins and discard the negative. We have a tendency to discount our wins and focus on the negative.

59. Be the first worker to step up and show compassion, concern and respect for your fellow employee.

60. An organization being open and honest with itself and its employees is an important step in "breaking through the four barriers to quality."

61. A company's honesty and integrity cannot be left up to interpretation by its employees.

62. Trust cannot be bought; it has to be earned day in and day out by every employee within the organization. Trust is the foundation for change.

63. Given the opportunity to help, people will help one another.

64. Wanting to belong is not an option—it is a need.

65. When given the opportunities, leaders will surface and rise to the occasion.

66. The bigger the organization, the less likely you are to consistently bump into that 1% bad employee within the organization. This gives that 1% employee the opportunity to wreak havoc on your organization. The employees must be encouraged to hold each other accountable and be supported for their efforts.

67. The hardest thing in regard to succession planning in the BaseWork Systems 2000 is the parent letting go of the business and letting his children assume the day-to-day responsibilities.

68. The integrity of your organization may not be reflected daily by your boss, so don't judge your organization too harshly.

69. The best way to deal with an employee that is holding the company hostage is to remove all emotion from the deal and manage, monitor, and hold him accountable. This employee will process himself out.

70. Being and saying you are of quality and being held accountable for quality are two completely different things. You cannot be quality until you can hold quality accountable.

71. That extraordinarily talented employee that you seek is probably already in your employment.

72. The best way to get started training an organization is: Make sure you are committed long term to training. Budget 2% - 6% of payroll for that training. Plan and schedule your training a year in advance and hold everybody accountable.

73. The only way training within your organization will succeed is with the total commitment and sign off of the owner/President/CEO and Board.

74. The quickest way to get the program moving is for the owner/President/CEO to step up and accept the responsibility and the burden for whatever is wrong in the organization. Now the company can move in a positive direction.

75. For training in an organization to be effective, everyone in that organization must receive job-specific training.

76. You cannot inspect quality into the product; you have to build quality into the process and system.

77. We are who we perceive ourselves to be.

78. A shut- down employee with potential is the biggest waste within an organization.

79. Let's become aware of how we communicate with one another and focus on the positive side of life.

80. Look out for new packaging of old concepts with no substance.
81. To have a continuously improving organization, the value and basis of the quality program must be reinforced daily.
82. The key to success is delegating to a formal, well-trained, and defined organization and having the trust in your organization to let go.
83. Your employee loyalty is not built overnight, and it can't be bought—it has to be earned.
84. Forget blame—focus on the solution and move on.
85. It takes greater strength internally to accept help than to give help when asked.
86. There is nothing more damaging to an organization and to a relationship than an employee of power with hidden agendas.
87. Only 1% of your organization does not welcome accountability.
88. Let's start a new fad that pays incentive bonuses for keeping employees, growing the business, and improving the process.

A Positive Note

Less than two percent of business problems are complex issues. The process to resolve the issues doesn't need to be complex either. There are employees internally, that with the proper training (removing the four barriers to quality) who can resolve those issues.

Bruce

APPENDIX A
Bruce Snell's Life Synopsis

Bruce Snell's Life Synopsis

At the age of 12 years, I came to the realization that I was a different kind of person. I began to realize that I was put on this earth to help people. That may sound corny or even egotistical, but it was how I felt. Even though I didn't know how, or what form helping people would take, I knew I was here for that reason.

Even in my early years, I questioned things internally. I kept them to myself, however, while trying to decipher what everything meant. When I would try to express thoughts to my peers, the looks and comments usually caused me to retreat inwardly.

I was a very happy person and felt tremendous love and respect for my father and mother. Both sides of my family were hard-working and good-hearted and possessed a strict sense of conscience, always trying to do what was right. I perceived myself very much like my family.

I seemed to get along better with older children and adults than with those my own age. I also sensed that most teachers didn't like me but those who did, did so passionately.

My mother always supported and defended my actions without hesitation. My daddy reinforced in me the need to stand up for what was right, to finish what I started, and to never run away from anything. He taught me to stand my ground and do what was right.

In grade school, I was a fighter and often got into trouble. My mother always went to bat for me. She took it upon herself to step in because Daddy worked two jobs and was absent much of the time. With five kids, there were times when Mom had to solicit Dad's help. He always tried to be there to support her.

Eighth grade was the biggest turning point in my life; I was asked to go out for our junior high football team. In order to play sports, I had to achieve academically in school. Soon, I started to look up to my coaches as being successful and I respected them for giving me direction and input. I had great rapport with my coaches starting in the ninth grade. I remember Coach McCory using me as an example of being tough, taking a hit, and standing firm. That made a great impression on me and built my self-esteem. To increase the quality of my performance, I would practice hours on end, until he made me stop.

I learned some early lessons from my daddy. He kept encouraging me to go out for basketball. I finally did and made the team. The lesson I learned was that a child, at an early age, sometimes can't make decisions. He must listen to and take advice from his elders/parents who can help him make sound decisions that might possibly affect other choices in life. I would later think about how close I came to not playing basketball, football, and baseball. Because of the encouragement of my daddy, basketball became my favorite sport both to practice and to play.

The next milestone in my life occurred during the high school years when I was playing football for Coach Bill Bacon. He was known by the students as being a tough disciplinarian. I went through those years never having a problem with the coach and developing a great respect for him. In reality, I became quite fond of him. Because of my lack of size at that time (I ultimately played football at 280 pounds), I listened and did exactly what he instructed me to do. In so doing, I became very sound in the fundamentals of football and ultimately team captain.

I tore all the ligaments in my ankle playing basketball my junior year causing me to miss football spring training. To catch up, I started running three miles a day. Once practice started, I was able to get back into shape. I was always in the top two to three running linemen.

One day everyone was complaining to Coach Bacon about the amount of practice, when he asked how much I had run before practice. I told him three miles. He said, "That's paying the price!" I hadn't thought anyone noticed, but apparently he did. It felt great!

Daddy always told me to be the first one on the field and the last one to leave. He said the coach would play someone who hustles. I never missed drills, practice, or school. I was always the first to volunteer and would hit until they pulled me out.

In my senior year I played both offense and defense and was on all the special teams. Because I was always soaked from head to toe with sweat running to the line and then back to the huddle, everyone thought I was too tired to go on. I always hustled, just like my daddy taught me. At one point, word got back to Coach Bacon that I needed a rest. He pulled me out of the game. I went to the coach and asked him why. He told me he thought I might need a rest. I told him that I had rested enough in my junior year. With that, he sent me back in the game and never pulled me again. I learned another lesson that night—work hard, do my job like I was asked, and if I paid the price, I would play.

I did well enough in high school, just getting by without really studying. Then I had college scouts starting to look at me. That meant college admission tests. To everybody's amazement, I did very well, actually scoring in the upper percentile.

Leaving home, I went to junior college at Marion Military Institute on scholarship in football, basketball and baseball. I worked hard and became a very good student and football player. After junior college, I went on to a four-year school on scholarship (Mesa State College in Colorado). During my junior year of college, I bought a house, I was working five part-time jobs, carrying a full business load, and playing football. Again, I had some great mentors and teachers. One whom I admired very much, Nick Anderson, took a special interest in me. When I would speak in class, other students would look at me and think I was crazy. Mr. Anderson, however, said I was "right on." He took the time to encourage me. He believed in me and made me believe I was of value; he continuously reinforced my self-worth. Mr. Anderson became my good friend and mentor. Again, I had learned a lesson: people will help but you have to ask, and if you are willing to pay the price, you will get the rewards.

I went on to graduate from Mesa State College in Grand Junction, Colorado. I had come a long way from my Alabama home. After college,

I was signed as a free agent for two years with the Denver Broncos. Those were the days of the "Orange Crush" defensive linemen in Denver. After trying out twice, I found I just didn't have the speed or strength to compete at that level.

Between the end of school and later working at a coal mine, I bought into a pizza place, working many hours with not much reward. Eventually, I fell out of the deal, but worked through it with my family and friends.

I worked at the coal mine on the belt lines where my job was to shovel coal when it fell off. During a second shift, I drove a truck. I worked hard and felt I was one of the best workers they had. Everyone else complained, but I was happy to have a job.

For two years, I ran wild and worked hard. Then I met the woman who is now my wife of many years, Karen Ordway. By then I was ready to move my life and career to the next step. Karen stepped up to the line and supported me both financially and emotionally while I tried different things.

I decided that I needed to move to California because Colorado was having tough times. My wife, Karen, and my good friend, Mark Harsha, lent me money to lease a new car. With $400 in my pocket, I headed for California to catch my dream.

On the way to California I stopped in Las Vegas and called my mother. She said she had friends in California and thought I could stay with them until I got my feet on the ground. I had planned on sleeping in my car and showering at a health club where a friend, Stan Fenn, had given me a membership. Instead, I stayed eight months with Grandma and Grandpa Leszinski and with Nancy and Bob Franz. These were very good people. The lesson I learned from this experience was that if you help a friend in need, you sow a good seed that will grow and bear the fruit of friendship that will last a lifetime.

My first job in California was data input for a commercial real estate company. When they asked if I could run/operate a computer, of course I said yes. Because of the hours I was willing to work, I learned my job and how to run the computer. I analyzed the job I was doing, deciding on the most logical way to collect data, download files and manage the data.

Within six months, our office was up and running well ahead of the other offices. Soon, I was asked to help open the Los Angeles office. I did so with great success, finding their needs different from the other offices. They needed a different software program.

Then I started to learn something the professors had never taught me in college, office politics. Some of the lessons I learned were:

1. Don't start off too fast because your co-workers take notice and it puts them on the defensive.
2. Keep to yourself; don't trust until it has been earned.
3. Management doesn't make the most logical decisions based on data, and some are insecure and have hidden agendas.
4. There is more involved in work than doing a good job at all levels.
5. It's easier to stay the same than to change.
6. Good work is noticed by both good and bad people.

I eventually went on to my next sales opportunity/job, after being unemployed for about 30 hours. In my first 18 months in commercial real estate, I worked 114 hours a week. Working around the clock, I sold during the day, and after work I did research, wrote letters, completed paperwork, and studied the business.

Almost every day I heard, "It's not how hard you work, but how smart." I was sick of hearing that! At that time I was spending about $10 to $15 a week on food and had $200 left in the bank. I soon closed my first deal and made enough money to live for a few more months (thanks Ken Smith!).

My colleagues made fun of me at sales meetings because I was spending too much time with my clients and needed to turn more deals. I didn't let that discourage me; I kept working hard and in a year I closed many deals and moved from Number 45 to Number 11 in the office while out-performing my rookie co-workers. The next year I finished as the Number one Broker and out of 2,000 brokers nationwide, I was in the top 16%.

After four years of closing many deals and making many friends, real estate was no longer rewarding or challenging. During all those years

I had been a team player, but for some reason real estate in Orange Country was not the team sport for me.

*I became very successful but did not feel fulfilled inside. A friend that I did business with was having a bit of trouble with his company. Sales were dropping after a steady climb. He asked me if I could help. That was the start of my "**life of quality**."*

A Positive Note

The employees and their company's state of well-being is directly affected by their perception, knowledge, understanding or insight concerning their daily interaction with the 4 barriers to quality.

Through BaseSkills Training the employee and company move to a higher level of awareness and judgment.

Bruce

APPENDIX B
Glossary

BaseWork Systems 2000©
DEFINITION OF TERMS

ACTION ITEM:

The action taken to perform any event. See **Action Item Form**. *We list who does what and hold everyone accountable.*

ACTION ITEM/QUICK ACTION FORM:

A form used to record the necessary information (actions, dates, names) to help the member/team complete the Action Item/quick action.

ADDITIONAL DUTIES:

These are the duties that are preformed in addition to our daily responsibilities and duties.

AGENDA:

A list of items to be dealt with at a meeting.

BaseValues:

The foundation of principles and rules that determines conduct and habit, which in turn affects all employees' welfare.

BaseWork Center© (BW/C)

A team member's area of expertise and control, his job.

BaseWork Systems© FILE:

File drawer is in the **BaseWork Systems©** *Room (lunch/break room). All forms and team files are kept there.*

BaseWork Systems 2000© INFRASTRUCTURING OF BUSINESS:

A quality program developed by working throughout the organization defining systems, processes and training needs. Employees are trained regarding the improvement/ agreement of the systems and processes. Every job (BW/C) will be defined and agreed on by the employee doing the job. Improve your work life and this will in turn improve your home life.

BaseWork Systems© MANAGEMENT:

Removing the fear of expression, opening up communication, defining procedure and the training of all above. Lighten up.

BaseWork Center© PROCEDURES FORM:

A form designed to assist the Task Team when writing a procedure. The final solution/ procedure will be written on this form and attached to the Task Team Form to be turned into the Coordinator.

BaseWork Center© PROCESS PACKET:

This is one of the first things the teams do. Start with a step-by-step of the BW/C.

BENCHMARKING:

A standard or point of reference in measuring or judging quality, value. Driving a stake into the ground, let's start from there.

BRAINSTORMING:

The process of generating a large number of ideas (problems, causes, solutions, etc.)

BREAK-EVEN:

Designating that point, as in a commercial venture, when income and expense are equal. Also a starting point.

BW/C # :

This number is assigned to every employee in the organization. The first two numbers represents location. The next six numbers are the department number and the last three numbers are the job within that department.

CAUSE:

The reason for; Why? Why does the problem exist?

CLARIFY:

To make clear.

CODE OF CONDUCT:

The rules we abide by during meetings and at work.

CONSULTANT/RESULTANT:

*A **Consultant** tells you what to do; a **Resultant** tells you how to do it.*

CONSENSUS:

All team members in agreement.

CONTROL CHARTS:

To verify by comparison with a standard or data collection. Set up in a diagram, table, graph, form.

COORDINATOR:

Serves as an administrator for the problem-solving process.

CROSS FUNCTIONAL:

Reaching from one BW/C to another; cross-training. From a task team problem-solving standpoint, people from different departments working on a task team to solve problems that affect them.

CROSS TRAINING:

Training a team member in a different **BaseWork Center**©. The best starting point is usually a job that is similar or your internal customer/supplier's BW/C. Give this a lot of thought; match skills.

DATA COLLECTION:

Facts and figures the team collects to support a problem, cause and/or solution.

DATA COLLECTION WORKSHEET:

A worksheet used to outline the collection of data.

DEALING WITH DATA:

Not making a decision or interpretation of an issue until you have received the facts, first-hand.

DEPARTMENTAL WALLS:

When one department cannot work with another due to hidden agendas or fear.

DIRECTED TASK TEAM:

Task Team that gets direction from the Steering Committee. Problems makes up 2-15% of Company's problems. (More complex)

DOING WHAT IS RIGHT:

When all else fails, do what is morally and ethically correct in making decisions.

EFFECT:

The result of a cause.

EMPLOYEE INVOLVEMENT (E.I.):

An organization that maintains the philosophy that all employees are encouraged to take ownership in their BW/C's (job).

EXTERNAL CUSTOMER:

Those who buy our finished product or service outside the company.

EXTERNAL SUPPLIERS:

Those from whom we get our supplies, parts, etc., from outside the company to do our jobs.

FACILITATOR:

They work "hands on" with the teams and help the leader with training and making sure things get done. Usually is BW/C supervisor or manager. Also has the responsibility of handling meetings.

FLOW CHARTING:

Showing steps in a sequence of operation.

FORMAL ORGANIZATION:

The agreement of process(s)/System(s) with in an organization by the employees that own that process(s)/System(s). By formalizing how we are doing business we create more flexibility and less anxiety for the employees.

FUNNEL CONCEPT:

The moving of the organization's employees to the point of acceptance of quality. Employees get involved at different times (jumping on). Less than 1% of employees within an organization are bad employees and those employees will remove themselves.

GOALS:

An object or end that one strives to attain.

GOALS IN CONFLICT:

When one BW/C's, department's, goals affect another in a negative way.

GRIPEITIS:

A person who sees everything in a negative way and volunteers to share it with whoever will listen. Usually is unhappy with himself. When confronted with the opportunity to resolve the issue, there is no issue; just an attitude problem.

HEARSAY:

Second-hand information that is usually without data or fact and meant in a negative way. The best way to handle is to put it in writing.

HIDDEN AGENDA:

To keep from others' knowledge of the real reason for your response. When responding a certain way that benefits you directly or indirectly at the expense of another.

HOLDING EVERYONE ACCOUNTABLE FOR QUALITY:

We do not accept or pass on non-quality from anyone. No personal or BW/C attacks— just resolve issues.

I.D. NUMBER:

Number given by the Coordinator to the Task Team before a team is started.

IMPLEMENTATION:

Putting the solution into practice.

IMPLIED PROCEDURE:

A way we believe our job is done; part or whole. (Not written)

INFORMATION CENTER:

The Company is broken into four Information Centers (I/C) Example: 1. Procurement

2. Production

3. Marketing

4. Administration

INTERNAL COMPLETION:

BaseWork Center, Departments and divisions competing against one another. This is usually set in place by quotas, incentives, bonus, performance merit day, piecework, etc. With internal compaction, one loses at the expense of the other. You are pitting one against the other and someone always has to lose.

INTERNAL CORRECTION:

By the organization improving internally what they control, external problems will be solved or in a position of improvement. Example: customers, suppliers, vendors, etc.

INTERNAL CUSTOMER:

Team members to whom we give our product/service or paperwork within our company.

INTERNAL SUPPLIERS:

Team members from whom we receive our work in our company. (Think: Product, Service, Paperwork)

LEADER:

A person who sets the example, walks the walk, talks the talk, guiding and helping, coaching his fellow team members. Promotes trust and fairness.

LINE ITEM MANAGEMENT:

The running of the business from the numbers alone. Usually an arbitrary number from the accounting reports. We are cutting expenses (line items) but not improving the way we are doing business. We are forgetting the relationship between quality and profits.

MANAGEMENT RESPONSIBILITY:

Management must lead the way to quality improvement because employees can't do it themselves. There must be strong commitment and direction. Management should give the total direction and monitor the direction being taken. Continuity improves the process and direction.

MONTHLY OVERVIEW:

Team leaders/facilitator fill out after the **BaseWork Systems**© meeting and turn into the Coordinator at the end of the second meeting each month.

MULTI-VOTING:

To rank the problems in the order that concerns most of the members to determine which problem(s) the team is going to work on.

NEGATIVE RAP:

A person that is involved in exchanging negative comments when communicating. Must be avoided. Think of how to communicate positively. Don't get caught up in the negative rap exchange.

OPEN AND HONEST COMMUNICATION:

When you can walk up to anyone in an organization and ask an open and honest question and get an open and honest answer.

POSITIVE NOTE:

Taking brainstormed problems or team members' thoughts and stating in a positive comment, and posted (for 30 days) at each location on the **BaseWork Systems**© Bulletin Board for all employees to read.

PREJUDICED PERCEPTION:

Viewing a situation/person and forming judgment or opinions based off past experiences before the facts/data are known.

PRESENTATION:

Step 5, Process A, Problem Solving. Is made to the approving entity—example, Steering Committee. Usually with the more complex problems.

PROBLEM STATEMENT:

To take the brainstormed problem and turn it into a Problem Statement that can be easily understood by anyone outside the group. A good problem statement usually suggests possible solutions.

PROBUS MANAGEMENT:

A Latin word for honesty and integrity.

PROCEDURE:

The sequence of steps to be followed. A good procedure is a written one.

PROCESS AND STEPS:

A process is something that you do and the steps of how you do them. This is like flowcharting.

PUT OUT FIRES:

Going day to day handling problems that reoccur from time to time due to lack of procedure (written), communication, training, etc.

QUALITY:

Excellence; superiority. Any feature that makes something what it is. Doing the right thing right the first time. The thing that makes us/company different and stand out in our industry and community.

QUALITY CONTROL:

A system/process for maintaining desired standards in product or process, not by inspecting but by building quality into the system/process.

QUALITY ISSUES:

Any violation of one of two guidelines:

1. *To do what is morally and ethically correct.*
2. *To treat everybody as you want to be treated.*

A quality issue can be because of process, procedure or people.

QUICK ACTION -PROCESS D:

Problems that can be resolved by a team without going through processes A, B or C. The team must reach a consensus agreement

RESOURCE PERSON:

A person that can answer questions from outside the scope of the team. This expert is usually invited to the meeting.

ROOT CAUSE:

The real reasons for the problem.

SPC: STATISTICAL PROCESS CONTROL:

Controlling or improving a system/process using data of that process/system. Dealing with data.

SPIN OUT:

When a team, working on Process A: Problem Solving reaches a consensus about the solution to the problem, they move to Process B: Task Team Format.

SPONSOR:

The person or Team that starts the action of a Task Team.

STEERING COMMITTEE:

*Responsible for direction and follow through for the **BaseWork Systems**© Program. Usually made up of upper and middle management.*

SYSTEM(S):

The company is built from BW/C to BW/C. When linked together by internal customer/ supplier you have system. System(s) are the way we do everything within the company. A system is made up of processes and steps linked together by internal customer/ suppliers.

TASK TEAM:

Teams of people who work together to complete a specific task. The members may include members of the **BaseWork Systems**© team (whole or part) and others from the different BW/C's for assistance. Members of the task team will still participate in their own **BaseWork Systems**© team meetings.

TASK TEAM LOG:

The accounting of all task teams by the coordinator.

TEAM LEADER:

A member of the team who leads the team through the **BaseWork Systems**© process by prepared agendas and follow-up with team members.

TQM: TOTAL QUALITY MANAGEMENT:

Means many things to many people but has to do with quality concepts (See **BaseWork Systems**©).

TRACKING:

Following the results of a solution put into action, or a trial test.

TRAINING/IMPLEMENTATION FORM:

Once a solution/procedure has been reached by a team/team member(s), the training/ implementation form is to be completed. The results are that all BW/C's affected by the solution receive training before the solution goes in to the BW/C's that are affected. Now the procedure is held accountable.

TRUST:

To allow to do something without fear of the outcome. A firm belief in honesty, integrity, reliability, justice, etc., of another person or thing. Most important emotion between a team member and organization.

VERBALLY VERIFY:

Verifying can be done without written data to support it. The team must reach a consensus.

WARNING NOTICE (EMPLOYEE):

A form used to notify the employee of their violation(s) of Policies and Procedures.

WHAT "IFING" THE DEAL TO DEATH:

When a deal is presented (put on the table) and before the deal is explained, we start "what if this or that happens"; "that sounds good, but what if?" Watch and see; before you know it you are at extremes with both sides of the deal what-ifing. Remember you should look at ways to support the deal from a positive standpoint.

WORKCENTER:

A workcenter is usually a more complex process/system that is one of perhaps many included under one BaseWork Center. This usually applies under office workers and management.

QUALITY WILL SHOW YOU THE MOST EXCELLENT WAY

Quality is patient, quality is kind. It does not envy, it does not boast, it is not proud. It is not rude, it is not self-seeking, it is not easily angered, it keeps no record of wrongs. Quality does not delight in evil but rejoices with the truth. It always protects, always trust, always hopes, always perseveres. Quality never fails.

Made in the USA
Columbia, SC
15 June 2018